THE REAL ESTATE BIBLE

HOW TO FOLLOW YOUR **HEART-LIGHT**

ALEX VASQUEZ

Printed in the United States of America

ISBN: 978-1-7340212-0-2

TESTIMONIALS

"

Everything throughout this book, Alex truly embodies. His unwavering approach to business and instinctual ability to connect you to key individuals, is all mapped out within these pages. But the true value Alex brings extends well beyond a business relationship, because his selfless, service first mindset, naturally radiates in his being.

—DARNELL & DANYEL JONES

Founders and Powerhandz, INC., EY Entrepreneurs Of The Year

Alex and I were friends long before business dealings came to the table. Our common passion for boxing is what bound us. When deals and negotiations did begin, the approach was as if we were still analyzing a great fight. In the business world, when someone can make such natural transitions and still deliver results, you know they are something special. Read the book and learn!

—ROB GARCIA **"**

Founder & CEO Braven Sport Combat Equipment,
Legendary Strength and Conditioning Coach

"

In the boxing world, everyone is out for something. It's well known that fighters tend to have to battle as much outside the ring with their business affairs, as they do during the actual fight. After working with Alex, I only regret not connecting with him earlier in my career. He brings a straightforward approach, is a handshake guy, and looks out for everyone's interests. If it's not win-win, he won't do it. Huge in today's world and a key component to any team looking to make real moves.

—AUSTIN "NO DOUBT" TROUT

WBA Super Welterweight Champion

Alex has made me and my family a lot of money. His mindset is that of a winner and his achievements in life are what backs that up. His attention to detail and relentless pursuit for win-win deals is why he succeeds. Coaching is an art in any platform and in regards to the Real Estate industry, Alex commands respect. The book will show you how you can attract what you want in life, without having to force it all the time. Don't pass it up!

—RYAN MILLER "

Assistant Head Coach, Texas Christian University

"

Life after the NFL is not easy. But with a friend and professional like Alex by my side, I have no choice but to succeed. His guidance and expertise has consistently helped me as I grow my new startup and enter the business world. Brothers for life!

—STEVENSON SYLVESTER **"**

4 Year NFL Career, Founder & CEO of KLYP

CONTENTS

ACKNOWLEDGEMENTS

W *riting a unique book about Real Estate is a challenge* and from the get-go I knew it had to be different to give value. I would like to thank all the people in my life for supporting me through this endeavor. When I decided to write this book, I accepted the commitment, and understood that it would teach me as much about myself as I am hoping to teach others. I realized that it would have to be born in an atmosphere of peace in both heart and mind. To my Mother, Pam, who inspired me in life and who should be on her tenth novel by now. This is the piece that will bring it all together.

To Amy, the love of my life. Your strength and courage to push forward gives me the will to do the same. All your work will liberate you as it continues to motivate me. I'll wait and will be with you in this life, or the next. Don't Forget.

To my Dad, I get it now. But I will forever miss you and for that reason I will never stop.

To my team, thank you for helping me grow into a man whose only fear is not giving it his all. Always moving forward is how it all started and how it will continue.

And, as ever, to God, who led me on the path of Love and guided my thoughts to this exact moment. Not sure where it's going to take me, but I've never worried too much about the destination, I just try and enjoy the ride ...

INTRODUCTION

'm the kind of person who consistently pushes the limits and looks for ways to better myself. Whether that is physically, mentally, emotionally or spiritually, I have always felt the best way for me to achieve great things is to continually grow and drive beyond my fears.

During a recent search for a new Real Estate book, I continually saw an unfulfilled niche. Sure, there was an abundance of books that showed me, "How to be the next millionaire in Real Estate" or books to teach me about, "The Real Estate boom", or "Real Estate made easy" and "The basics of Real Estate". I felt like I'd read them all. However, as I continued my search, I realized the key element that I learned from many successful individuals in real estate, had been left out.

A gap in the market perhaps? I thought so ...

It seemed to me that the core of what turns dreams into reality and allows your fears to subside, had somehow been overlooked. Let me explain. I'm not referring to a hidden secret or a get rich quick scheme. I used the word "bible" in the title of this book, knowing it carries a religious connotation, and it can be correctly assumed that God, or a higher being, is the cornerstone of this book's foundation.

My objective is not to preach or sway you towards a particular faith, but to encourage you to embrace your own inner light. And to help you blend this real-life "superpower" with your Real Estate business and day to day activities. That is the niche I feel has been missed — until now. In my experience, the individuals who rise to the top all have one thing in common: they believe in something bigger than themselves, and while they are committed to excellence to an almost manic degree, and love the rewards that come with those efforts, they clearly go about their work with a sense of purpose. Being able to do what they love naturally paves the pathway to success. And coincidentally, the financial aspect of success tends to be a part of that. In this book, I will guide you to discover a way of being will give you a sense of personal freedom and, if implemented, can far exceed anything money can buy. My aim is to give you practical tools to unlock your true being and genuine nature. Having happiness and passion for what we do is pure liberation, and I believe it is something we all deserve.

I hope you're ready to walk down this path and give yourself everything God intended you to have. We work the majority of our lives, therefore we might as well embrace it, otherwise our true gifts will never fully shine.

I want to jump straight into the heart of the book, but before I do, I have a quick story I want to share with you.

I was running my Real Estate brokerage when I was approached by the local managing partners of Berkshire Hathaway: Warren Buffett's company. One of the partners was a close friend and mentor. They had watched my company grow and they made an offer to acquire my firm. The acquisition was based on my company's future trajectory and Berkshire Hathaway's intention to expand their market share.

My fledgling company was in its infancy when they approached me. Initially, my business plan had been to build the brand to the level where I would franchise it myself. However, when the offer was made to buy, I felt I had no choice but to weigh out the options. To be honest, I was honored and in awe that this world-renowned brand was taking an interest in my company, and in me. I took it as a huge compliment and I was extremely flattered. With all of this in mind, I concluded that accepting their offer was the best decision and we proceeded to get the deal closed.

Part of the terms were for me to help the managing partners run the two hundred plus brokerage firm: from culture influencing, to recruiting, to marketing. Once the ink was dry on the contract, I hit the ground running and worked non-stop for eighteen months straight! Afterwards I took a vacation for a couple of weeks, and while it was a celebratory trip, looking back, I think it was more to clear my head and recharge my batteries from the huge workload that initially ensued.

"Did it change my life?" For sure it built my notoriety and credibility, and I was nominated and awarded for several achievements; including the "40 Under 40 Award". From a financial standpoint it positioned me to scale my other business and grow my personal Real Estate portfolio. But most importantly, it gave me the opportunity to provide for my family and loved ones. I am truly grateful for such an amazing chapter in my business life and this book is my way of giving back.

Thank you for joining me on this incredible adventure: if you are ready, let's begin and, most importantly, let's have some fun!

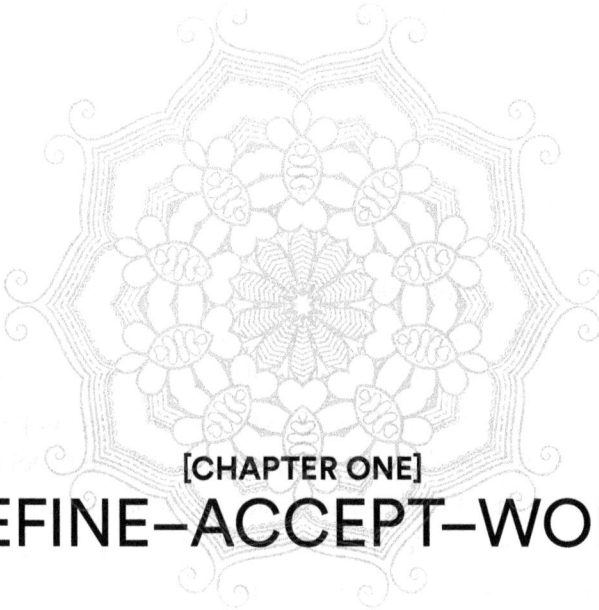

[CHAPTER ONE]
DEFINE–ACCEPT–WORK

n my experience, and I wholeheartedly believe this to be true, when we clearly define what we want, and when we totally accept our circumstances, and when we are entirely prepared to work all-out, relentlessly, then absolutely nothing can stop us from achieving our dreams.

I was taught that timing was everything. I heard it everywhere, so I believed it to be true. When I first set out, I didn't recognize what I know now, and even if I did, I doubt I would change a thing. I believe it was the tough times that enabled me to experience the good times. Looking back over my shoulder to ponder my highs and lows, they've merged to form a flow of true-life experiences. And, that's true for all of us. I entered the Real Estate market in 2006, right before the market tanked. Everyone was leaving, running for the hills, just as I was marching in. The timing was terrible, but timing is everything!

When the whole world around you seems to be caving in and abandoning ship, you're left with one obvious option: to move forward!

So that's what I did. I defined, I accepted, and I worked.

I took the decision to make the shift from my busy career in hospitality, into Real Estate. My time as a chef had come to an end, and now it was the stage for me to pursue my destiny. I believe cooking taught me how to work extremely hard. When you're working behind a blistering hot stove in a kitchen for fourteen hours a day, six days a week, in uncomfortable, difficult conditions, you build up your reserves of endurance most others can't fathom.

As a chef, I was on a comfortable salary, so at twenty-three I purchased a new house, bought a new car, and a five-acre plot of land. Naturally, that was with the understanding my salaried chef position was going to sustain all of these acquisitions. When I transitioned into Real Estate, it was a completely commission-based role. I got my Real Estate licence and I was ready, but like most new brokers entering the business, what I needed was a steady income until my new trade proved profitable. I worked at the Olive Garden waiting tables at night, Tuesday through Sunday. During the day, I worked at Foot Locker part-time.

About two years in, I got rid of the Foot Locker job, but I continued to wait tables for six years while working my Real Estate business. I was very fortunate because the manager of the restaurant was a good friend, and it enabled me to work deals while I was running tables. A typical evening looked like this: I would serve bread and drinks to new customers, then I'd get a text or an email. I'd run to the back, call, and start negotiating, and begin writing up contracts on my phone. It was a very humbling lesson. Today when I put on a suit and tie, and actually go out and just talk to people, I have no room to complain at all.

For six years my life was nothing other than waiting tables, writing Real Estate contracts, clearing tables, reading emails, serving drinks, and working deals. There was no order to the play list, just work, lots of hard work.

My first home was a 2,000 square-foot, four-bedroom house. It was too big for me alone. I decided to rent out the rooms for $600 a room, and I did that for eight years. I made a profit of $600+ per month on my own house. Each night I came home to essentially a damn frat house in order to pay the bills. This is just one example of the sacrifice I made to obtain success. I worked sixteen-hour days to survive, I had to. Today, I work sixteen-hour days because I want to.

> 66
>
> **Your new path, the one that allows you to break free from what you're doing, can often come from right under your nose, when you least expect it.**
>
> 99

Your new path, the one that allows you to break free from what you're doing, can often come from right under your nose, when you least expect it.

The general manager, who was my friend from the Olive Garden, bought his retirement home, which was close to a million-dollar transaction. Coincidentally, in the same month, I closed another million and a half dollars multifamily complex. Which I also double ended: in Real Estate terminology that means you represent both the buyer and the seller. In this instance, it was a bank owned property that they wanted to offload and on that commission alone, I made in excess of $75,000. Added to the commission from the Olive Garden General Manager million-dollar deal, I pocketed a shade under $100,000.

My six-figure month enabled me to leave the Olive Garden and tackle my Real Estate business full-time, safe in the realization I had a comfortable nest egg. $100,000 in one month! But remember, that was six years in the making.

Whilst I juggled my Olive Garden work alongside my business, I managed to become a multimillion dollar Real Estate producer. My first full year I sold thirty houses and then consistently thirty to fifty houses per year. If you sell $2 million worth of Real Estate that makes you a multimillion dollar producer. In terms of compensation you need to look at the numbers. So, let me break it down.

Commissions average between 3% and 6% depending if you double end. Let's say 4% is the average. For every million dollars of Real Estate you sell you make $40,000. From that you pay a brokerage fee that can range anywhere from 30% to 50%, you have to pay for your license, your marketing and expenses. If you take $20,000 home you're fortunate. In broad strokes, if you sold $5 million of Real Estate you should be making roughly $100,000 per year.

That's not a terrible living, but it's nowhere near what the media portrays. There's a reality to Real Estate. It has taken me over ten years to sell in multiples of ten, twenty and thirty million dollars' worth of Real Estate.

Let's drill down into the core of this chapter and explore Define, Accept, and Work.

DEFINE

The Oxford Dictionary definition of "Define" is: *state or describe exactly the nature, scope or meaning of.*

'I want to be successful.'

You tend hear that statement all the time. And it's accurate to say that most people want to be successful, but that alone is not a goal. Without a target and a defined agenda, the majority of people will fall short of their dreams. In order to turn your dreams into goals, and your goals into manageable, attainable targets, you need a systematic, religious approach. Without it, you'll flounder. I see it too often. Every day you must strive to dedicate your best intentions to what you seek.

In Real Estate, you must define where you wish to focus your energies. However, there is a crucial step you must consider first. Ask yourself, "Is this career choice my heart's desire?" Follow up by asking yourself, "Do I see myself working to help others through God or a higher purpose, to create value and wealth for all parties involved?" And, "Can I have fun in this career? Is this a win-win for everyone?"

These are powerful, soul searching, yet simple questions, designed to compel you to decide whether the Real Estate business is the path for you.

Consider this: if you are going into real estate thinking you'll be closing million dollar deals every month, dressing up stylishly to take clients out to eat in nice restaurants a few times per week, and driving a fancy car from deal to deal then I need to warn you ...

Unless you have a solid financial foundation in place, or a vast network of motivated buyers and sellers ready to go, or you are inheriting a successful book of business, then you have something very different coming to you.

Real Estate is no different from any other business: if you are working from the ground up then it will be tough, cut-throat, and most will fail or struggle to get by.

I've seen bright, confident, energetic people who are capable of success, tackle this industry, and yet, within a few months they realize it is nothing like they imagined (deals, lunches, fast cars) and begin to question their decision to get started.

Here's why.

The majority of people in Real Estate are independent contractors. They have no pre-set schedule or mandated office hours. They are free to come and go as they please; and for many, this is a dream position. An occasional staff meeting with your Qualifying Broker, and nobody telling you what to do, when to do it, and how to do it. I know many people who dream of this scenario. The problem is this, if you do not follow a well thought out schedule, a routine that you can execute daily, then you'll spend days, weeks, months and in some cases whole careers making little headway.

If you are unprepared to create and follow a productive plan of action, then you're better off in a nine-to-five program where you at least know you'll be receiving a monthly pay check. The Real Estate business is high risk with the possibility of high reward. And while thankfully there is no ceiling, you'll soon learn that your inner strength is the key to pushing through the inevitable emotional roller coaster each new deal brings.

Defining *your* niche: The beauty of this business is that once you are licensed there are countless paths you can follow. There are key areas in real estate including, residential sales, commercial sales, flips, and property management. Furthermore, there are a wide range of reality TV shows spotlighting real estate projects and ideas which receive a lot of exposure. I have encountered successful brokers who consult for major companies, and these same deals ended up earning them a seven-figure payday. Remember, real estate offers endless opportunities, and everything is negotiable.

Having clarity will help define the direction you wish to take. There is a huge contrast between residential and commercial, property management, and property development. They're all different facets of real estate, so defining what it is that you want to do is a major part. For example: the difference between a commercial broker and a residential broker is like night and day. Defining what you want to do is often based on what's in front of you. If you live in a town of five hundred people, and you think you're going to sell one hundred homes a year, you should drastically adjust your expectation.

I live in Albuquerque, New Mexico, with a population of roughly two million people in the whole state. When you look at it from a financial perspective, there are not a lot of million-dollar homes. The average price point of a house is $240,000, and that, from a compensation standpoint, is about $6,000 per house sale. Doing the same work, essentially the same job: writing the same contract, in LA,

New York, Chicago, D.C., where a million-dollar sale is not unusual, your commission is $30,000 per deal. Same work, $24,000 difference. Understanding and then clearly defining what your market represents is vital for you to realize your full potential.

I'm an independent contractor, so I only get paid when I produce. My knowledge base, my education, comes from my efforts in expanding what I know. As a broker, if you sit looking at the wall, you're not gaining anything, you will not move forward. You have to take action, you have to cold call, you have to read real estate books, you have to stay up with trends, you have to attend seminars and networking events. To make it count, you've got to define what you want to do. I know some people who spend hours and hours reading about selling beachfront property. Why would I do that? I don't have a beach, I live in the desert. Some people think they need to read everything, master everything. It's crucial to accept that a lot of things we must do are not fun. Reading the wrong things can be as damaging to you as not reading at all.

I often hear brokers complain they haven't hit their goals. When I ask why, I quickly see from what they say that their niche is disconnected from their goal. For example: they live in a town with two hundred properties and they aim to sell fifty per year. Another misjudgment is when brokers do not compare apples with apples. This is especially true when comparing residual and commercial real estate results.

Dave says, 'I sold twenty-five houses this quarter and made less in commissions than Sandra who only sold two commercial properties.'

Across the country, and the world, you can assume that the price of a commercial building is far higher than that of a residential property and it would be obvious to see the commissions reflected in that as well. Brokers easily get frustrated fighting this uphill battle. Giving yourself a level playing field to compete and attain your goal is paramount. Selling twenty-five homes per quarter (which is admirable by the way) can be just as complex as selling two commercial buildings. Remember, apples to apples.

Defining your niche and making a plan, and then sticking to it, is the only true real estate formula. The next question I get asked is, "How long should I stick to my plan before I modify or scrap it altogether?" Unfortunately, in real estate there are too many niches and factors to give you a clear answer. It's part gut-feel, part experience, and part trial and error. However, as your experience grows, your judgement will improve and your gut-feel will fine tune in its accuracy. You cannot replace experience with anything.

> **Defining your niche and making a plan, and then sticking to it, is the only true real estate formula.**

ACCEPT

The Oxford Dictionary definition of "Accept" is: *to consent to receive or undertake.*

What does accepting mean to you? Your answer to that question will be the major factor in determining how you are willing to reach your goals. Notice, not "if" but "how" you are going to reach your goals. Reaching your goals is about "how", not about "if". A great quote comes to mind, "Every man dies, not every man really lives." To wholeheartedly accept one's choices is to be at peace, and unattached to the outcome. Whatever the outcome, anticipated or not, you must allow yourself to be free and have peace knowing that each step gets you closer to your goal. Without this base-level understanding, most people go through life as a victim and never take accountability of the most important tool at their disposal ... choice.

Buddha said, "Pain is not a choice, suffering is."

In Real Estate, pain could translate as a multi-million-dollar deal imploding days before completion. To make matters worse, let's say it was a double-end deal, twofold commission up in smoke, gone. For some this could derail them not just financially but also mentally and emotionally. Sometimes indefinitely. I experienced a deal rather similar to this and the rest of the year was not the same. You may not have had that occurrence yet, give it time, and you will, I promise. These experiences are lessons for us to learn, what we need to learn in order for us to evolve.

Breakthroughs typically come following a business or life breakdown. Defeat is always followed by the lesson. It's life's way of teaching us to grow. For any of us to obtain success, our goals and our faith in the universe must be more powerful than our pain and fear. You must find the way to keep moving, let go, and accept. Do it now, do it later, but either way you have to do it.

Those who hold on and can't accept, grow bitter and angry. They blame the world and fail to open their hearts to the true potential that can only exist when you accept what is, forgive, let go and move on. And when you do, the next lead, the next deal, the next closing, is exactly what you need at that exact right moment in your life. The universe is not conspiring against you, it's working with you, offering you lessons, showing you the way. And yes, it's hard. I know!

To accept the outcome will keep you ahead of the vast majority. While they will be questioning why something happened, looking to blame, focusing on the past, you will already have moved on. As they waste time on "what ifs", you are open to the present moment, ready to receive all the amazing opportunities life has in store for you. Dwelling closes the heart, which closes doors. Moving forward opens the heart and allows prosperity.

The formula: accept, analyze effectively, learn the lesson—move on.

The key is to learn. Only to move on is a fool's errand. Learning is the key. Bill Gates said, 'Success is a lousy teacher. It seduces smart people into thinking they can't lose.' Wise words. I've found that success and failure are equal teachers. Some experiences leave a lasting imprint and make it hard for us to move on. As hard as you try to accept and progress, the grip of the experience won't leave you. The problem you face when you do not truly accept and push forward, is that the experience can define you. This can become a crippling definition and stunt your future potential.

Once a pinnacle of success has been reached, some, not everyone, begin to put themselves above others, while others stop the process of developing and expanding. Due to their success, they somehow feel entitled.

So, I repeat: accept, analyze, move on.

Truly successful people accept God was just as much a key factor in leading them to greatness, and understanding this truth is what makes them thrive and keeps them grounded when the tides turn. Accept failure, accept success, analyze and move on.

A middle ground exists between success and failure: standard, just good enough, being OK. It exists because it is easier to accept than the highs and lows of triumph and disappointment. Michelangelo said, "The great danger for most of us lies not in setting our aim too high and falling short, but in setting our aim too low and achieving our mark." It is after all, comfortable to live in the shadowlands of mediocrity and accept the status quo of society's lower standards.

To become a high producer in real estate is rare, it's not the norm. Accepting failure, accepting your big deal falling apart, will help you get past it. Bear in mind that you will face many failures. Failure is part of life, you cannot cut it out, because life tends to throw at you what you can handle. Today, when I'm facing hard and difficult times, sometimes I rewind the tapes of how life used to be. I was working three jobs, Foot Locker by day, waiting tables by night, and with a house full of roommates. In between I'd do all I could do to procure real estate deals. After the reflection, it is always hard for me to complain.

Acceptance is a huge challenge for everyone. I don't think it gets easier, I believe that challenges in life grow to the size of the person's ability to endure them. Meaning, the stronger we are, the more life will test you. Instead of feeling sorry for a major struggle in your world, look at it as an opportunity that you must be ready to tackle. We must grow to meet the challenge. What once stopped us is now no longer an issue. From the outside looking in, it is hard to see ourselves grow, but those observing from the inside looking out, start to see the growth and how it changes the challenges in life. Once you accept and forgive, then you truly are free.

WORK

Definition: *"I don't count my sit ups; I only start counting when it starts hurting because they're the only ones that count."* —Muhammed Ali

It is not a common phenomenon to be driven to success. Some say being driven is a blessing. It's like having a non-stop fuel supply to an engine. Many people desire to achieve greatness in Real Estate, however, when they come to realize the sacrifice required to turn their dreams into reality, very few have the means to endure. I have learned that sometimes we need to be just as driven to learn the discipline to turn off, and stop work.

Have you attended a motivational seminar, or had a great workout at the gym, and said to yourself, "Today is the day I'm going to start working on my goals to accomplish my dreams." But, within a week you are back to your old routine. The problem is, that most people are expecting a sprint to success with their new found posture of motivation. They are not prepared for the reality that achievement is not a sprint, or a quick burst, it is a marathon. When your sole focus is only on the endgame, you often ignore the path you're taking to get there. The few who do make it, often arrive burnt out and numb. Their goal, that was once their purpose, became nothing more than a to do list to check off. How you work is crucial, more simply put: there are no shortcuts.

I have always been ambitious. During summer at high school I started a landscaping company, during winter I ran a Christmas light installation business. It was normal for me to pack in as many jobs as I could and work as much as possible. I remember, back then Air Jordans were the "must have" item, so I had to have a pair for the first day of school. I would work from five am to six pm, Monday through Friday, (weekends too if I could secure the work). Because of my flat-out pace, summer soon came to an end and the start of school was approaching. I had made good money and was happy with my earnings, and as a result, was one of the few kids in my class, a proud owner of a new pair of Air Jordans, but I was always reluctant to transition back into school full-time. I was loving my business and my work, where had the summer gone?

Today, in the Real Estate business, I find myself being pulled into the same mindset; work, work, work. To this day I still have to make clear intentions to create the right balance. I see too many brokers with the attitude that getting as many properties under contract and closing, is more important than anything else in life. To outdo your numbers from the previous month or quarter can be motivating, yet in my mind, can also be a blinding dynamic of the business.

> ❝
> I regularly remind myself to
> enjoy the journey,
> as I continue to grind hard.
> ❞

From the client's perspective, how secure would you feel if you were viewed, by your broker, only as a number on a sales chart? Hard work, the hustle, the grind, the non-stop effort, can seemingly be an acceptable excuse to justify the disconnect, not only with our clients but with ourselves. And I understand the mechanics ... the more business you push into the pipeline, the more sales, the greater success, then the harder it is to stay connected with each client. This taught me one thing: That you need to acknowledge, fairly quickly, when your business reaches this stage. Otherwise the longer you wait, the harder it will be to try and reestablish rapport. I would urge you to reach out and connect with your clients who you personally work with. Embrace them as a true blessing and make them feel human and not a stat for that quarterly sales goal. I've found when I do this, my world slows down to a manageable speed and life pours back into my soul. A necessary for me and my clients and what becomes a win win for everyone.

I regularly remind myself to enjoy the journey, as I continue to grind hard. Always a work in progress, I have to keep an eye on myself and bring balance to my life, all the while embracing the path of my journey. I truly believe that hard work is a key ingredient of achieving amazing success. The process of reaching your goals is just as precious as the goal itself. Without your goal, you have no journey, without your journey, you won't realize your goals. They are entwined from beginning to end.

Keeping your eyes on the prize and just focusing on the outcome, is nothing more than a trap. It's an easy one to justify into and remain. In doing so we fail to acknowledge the dedication, commitment, sacrifice and discipline it takes to achieve anything worthwhile. This mindset continually sets us up for unrealistic expectations, which leads ultimately to disappointment. Great achievements take time, so be gentle on yourself and know that each brick you lay gets you that much closer.

It is a commonly held belief that 10,000 hours is what it takes to make you a master. I'm twelve years in and believe it when I say, I've got at least fifteen years to go, in terms of where I see myself being a real estate "Jedi". The future looks promising and I'm very excited about the passage ahead. You won't find me sitting around saying, 'Hey, I'm a decade in, I've gone way beyond the magical 10,000 hours marker, so why don't I have this, or that, and the other?' The faster you can accept the path takes years and years, the more you will be able to enjoy the ride.

Work smart, not hard.

You hear this one all the time too. I think it has a tendency to create laziness in those looking for a shortcut to avoid the work. But there is a huge element of truth to it that also cannot be denied. Lord knows you need to work hard in order to understand what working smart means. If you don't work hard, and bust your ass, and fail on numerous occasions, then you'll never know what working smart feels like. You'll have no yardstick, no barometer, no way of knowing.

The concept of failing is great, it's your biggest lesson, it's giving you the chance for you to say, 'OK, I get it.' However, it's crucial to fail as fast as you can, because sometimes failure is not recoverable. Especially as you begin to scale; your reputation, your performance is not negotiable, and if you promote yourself as a premier product, and then you come up short, it's hard to recover from that.

Without sounding redundant, working very, very hard in

everything you do, allows you to work smarter. It can allow you to implement systems and tools that make your operations tighter and more efficient. Typically, you never get away from hard work, if you're truly evolving all of the time, and working smarter is only the result of working hard. Working hard is the backbone for all you achieve, and those who follow this mandate rarely fall short of their goals.

Defining, accepting, and working are the three inescapable truths of success. Trust me when I say, "Avoidance behavior leads to failure." There are no shortcuts. I've seen people who fight against it, and I've seen people who attempt to forge a different pathway, and many who simply ignore the work factor. But, in the end there is no disputing. The three pillars of truth are incontrovertible: Define, Accept, and Work.

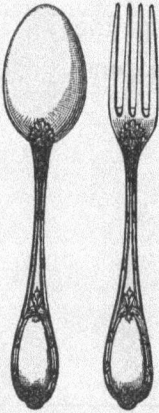

[CHAPTER TWO]
EAT–SLEEP–PRAY

want to invite you into the heart and soul of my world. Getting closer
to a purer existence starts with the basics of eating, sleeping and
praying. And, it couldn't be simpler, and it couldn't be harder, both at
the same time.

To a few, eat-sleep-pray comes through them as a natural gift. For
them it's innate, something they are born with, not unlike someone
who is outstanding in sport. But, for the many, myself included, eat-
sleep-pray is a learned experience, a new way of feeling, and a new
way of living.

Eat-sleep-pray has a depth that few other subjects can manifest.
It could be a stand-alone series of books and seminars all of its own.
There is no substitute, and no workaround to absorbing this belief and
way of being. Furthermore, while it is something you learn, it is far
more about who you become.

Eating a nutritious diet and getting sufficient sleep is essential for
physical health and mental resilience. Whilst we all know this, few do
it. I also encourage you to consider integrating prayer or a spiritual
practice of your choice into your daily routine. The impact on your
mind, body, and spirit is a powerful one.

Let's dive into the specifics of Eat, Sleep and Pray.

EAT

"To Eat is a necessity but to eat intelligently is an art."—Francois De La Rochefoucauld

Someone once told me that you couldn't expect to look or perform like a million bucks when you eat off the dollar menu. That really stuck with me. Each time my temptation for crappy food took over, I would do my best to revert to that wisdom. My first career choice as you now know was in the food world. With a degree in culinary arts, I was blessed with the ability to create the most gut-busting, calorie filled, fat-laden cuisine. Fortunately, as a chef and personal trainer, I also had the nutritional know how and personal experience to put together custom meal plans. I went from a diet consisting of cereal, donuts, energy drinks, pizza, and crème brûlée (in my early 20s) to the polar opposite when I was training for an all-natural bodybuilding contest. I have stood at all angles of the food pyramid. The bodybuilding regimen was hell because I had to eat as much as 5000 to 6000 calories a day, which were limited to a very few high protein, low carb and sugar items: broccoli, yams, protein shakes, tilapia, and never-ending chicken.

I discovered the best regimen for a balanced, healthy meal plan only after I began to listen to and understand my body. From that point on I noticed how much more energy I had when compared to most others. I could peel off fifteen-hour days, six days a week and didn't feel tired.

How does this pertain to Real Estate? We're in a time where instant gratification is the new normal and we expect everything yesterday. One of the most neglected aspects of our society is how we eat. With regards to Real Estate, as the transactions get bigger, more complicated and more frequent, your ability to perform is directly related to how good you feel. And how well you feel is affected by how you eat. Your nutritional intake sets you apart from the competition. For example, Broker A stuffs his face with a Double Quarter Pounder with cheese and French Fries, but Broker B chooses a meal that provides their body with healthy nutrients and sustainable energy. When it comes crunch time who do you think will prevail? I don't know about you, but I'd put my money on Broker B. It's hard to consistently beat someone whose mind and body are firing on all cylinders.

It's true what they say; life is a marathon, not a sprint. The point is, most people are not playing for the end game, they are doing what's convenient in the moment. It takes discipline to eat healthily and it's true when people say it's a lifestyle.

Success in Real Estate takes work and our diet is one of the few things we can control. A few simple shifts in what you eat can separate you from the pack. This ability to embrace a healthy lifestyle will enable tremendous and measurable results. In my opinion, ninety days, (Not thirty!) is the barometer to see significant results, so patience is required but the pay-off is worth it. Anything less than ninety days isn't enough time and doesn't give your body sufficient chance to make the shift. I won't go into meal plans or work out regimes here (maybe in my next book) but I will give you a few life hacks that have saved me when my dollar menu craving kicked in.

Snack Packs

I'm not talking about the pudding! My definition of a snack pack is a daily filled assortment of fresh fruit, vegetables and low sugar and carb filled meal replacement supplements, such as bars and shakes. These are great foods to keep you satisfied throughout the day, specifically between meals.

When a client is only in town for the day and wants to see houses at lunch time, duty calls. But your food intake doesn't have to suffer. Bring enough for two and offer your client a healthy option. They may decline, but it's a great icebreaker and puts you in a favorable light. And if they accept, the added bonus is they'll have more energy to view houses and to enjoy their time with you. Enthusiastic prospects more frequently convert into happy clients than starving, low energy ones.

Eating Schedule

When and how often you eat is equally as important as what you eat.

Picture this, you have been up since 5am and after your morning workout you were able to put together a nice breakfast before your day. Awesome start. But, your first meeting at 8.30am runs over by thirty minutes and your 10am gets pushed back to 11am. Then your 11.30am showing gets moved to 12.30pm and before you know it, it's 4pm and you haven't been able to eat. This is a typical day in Real Estate. 5pm rolls around and you're desperate to stuff your face with whatever's available. In those weak moments, you consume more calories than in the two previous days combined. Then at 9pm just before you had planned to go to sleep, your stomach growls and you justify a large bowl of cereal or a leftover Panini. After all, it's been a long, hard day and you're hungry. Sound familiar? For most of us in the real estate business, eating regularly isn't something that comes naturally.

Taking the time to schedule your food intake is a great habit to develop, which helps keep your energy and focus consistent. It may sound basic, but setting up an automated calendar reminder, to serve as a gentle prompt for you to eat at designated times throughout the day is helpful. This can be the difference between eating healthily and going too long without eating so you lose control.

I have found that eating at least five small meals and snacks versus two or three large servings, keeps me on my game. I recommend that you experiment with what works for you.

Networking Events

It's usual for a morning networking event to provide bagels, donuts and coffee. A lunch event may offer pizza or club sandwiches, with potato chips and soda. An afternoon networking event might serve cheese, crackers and kettle corn. Evening networking events frequently offer an open bar and high calorie snacks such as cream cheese pinwheels, followed by cake or cookies for dessert.

Welcome to the food world of the real estate broker! After a couple of months of eating like this you can see why a broker's waist is liable to jump up by three or four sizes.

There are many issues with this current food fiasco. The first which is the most apparent, but in my opinion, the one you should worry about least, is feeling like an outcast when you don't eat crap. Just find the right balance for you. There's no point worrying why someone chooses to eat 1500 calories before 10am, simply do your best to be non-judgmental and that way you won't alienate people.

Don't waste your networking time trying to convert people to your food choices. My advice is to stick to your own plan and enjoy networking.

The next challenge is how to supplement your food intake when faced with back-to-back or all-day events. The only solution I have found that works for me is to plan meals and/or healthy snacks in advance. It's easy to pull out a protein bar or piece of fruit during a break. Fresh pastries and donuts are tempting, but in the long run it's not going to keep you burning the critical clean fuel.

If you don't have what you need with you, it's usually possible to sneak out for a quick break to buy something. If leaving is out of the question, the best thing to do is to modify what's available. Typically, you will get a three-course meal that includes a salad with your choice of dressing (Ranch or vinaigrette), bread, a main course (protein, veggie, starch) and a dessert. The salad with vinaigrette is a go, pass on the bread and enjoy the protein and veggie. If you eat the starch; mashed potatoes are sometimes hard to pass up, then avoid dessert.

My Achilles heel is my sweet tooth, so if I crave dessert I'll pass on the starch in my entrée.

Ultimately you will have to do your best to navigate the perils of food during business networking. It's worth finding what works for you because it will position you ahead of the competition.

SLEEP

"Sleep is the golden chain that binds health and our bodies together."
—Thomas Decker

Sleep has been one of the most challenging aspects of keeping my mind and body at peak performance. My former career as a chef called for long hours and late nights and this meant that typically any social activity only happened after midnight. When I transitioned into Real Estate, the formula of waking up at dawn did not appeal to me. I wasn't particularly late to bed and definitely wasn't an early riser. I enjoyed my nights, and liked to wake up around eight or nine o'clock and felt that I was most productive with this sleep schedule.

After years of trying to maintain my old regimen in the Real Estate world, I realized how drastically my energy shifted once I became an early riser. This shift lead to more productivity and consistency in both my workouts and business, which in turn lead to more sales.

I found the early bird does catch the worm, but do be conscious that most humans need at least eight hours of sleep. As much as you may want to be a machine and take pride in the fact that you only sleep for four hours each night, this path will not lead you to the Promised Land. In most cases it will lead you to the ER! This is exactly what happened to me. We get caught up in the celebrity hype that preaches that waking up at the crack of dawn is part of the formula to outwork the competition. One article I read reported that Mark Walberg is up at 3am. I'm not saying that being an early riser isn't advantageous, what

I'm saying is that most real estate brokers are not pulling in twenty million per transaction and it's not necessary to work through the night.

The point is that we need to be realistic about our life and our body and what makes sense for both. It's great to be inspired by celebrities but don't forget that you are not that person.

> 66
>
> ## The bottom line is to identify the schedule that works consistently well for you.
>
> 99

The real question is: what is right for you? Whether you have a family or you are single will have an obvious impact on your sleeping patterns. Are you working several jobs to cover your bases as you transition to full-time Real Estate, or are you able to jump into the business full-time? These variables will make huge impacts on both your sleep quality and quantity. To sustain my lifestyle and workout regimen with sufficient clean fuel to burn, I must get a solid eight hours of sleep. Only after I tested my limits of trying to function well on fewer hours, did I come to the conclusion that my number is eight. I'm now more aware of my personal and professional time commitments and although at first it may seem limiting, but adequate sleep really does enhance your quality of life. This awareness keeps you accountable, makes you more organized and leads to you being more efficient.

In today's fast-paced world, a pre-workout before the gym, a quad espresso from Starbucks before breakfast and a couple of energy drinks after lunch, are not usual behaviors to try to keep up with the frantic pace. Although these quick fixes may work in the short term, this lifestyle isn't sustainable and can cause you to crash and burn.

The bottom line is to identify the schedule that works consistently well for you. Consistency is the key. I have found that between 5am and 6am is my ideal wake up time. Later than that tends not to provide me with the most opportunity to maximize my day. For those who dread the morning, it won't be easy, but I guarantee you will start to see positive results in your Real Estate career.

PRAY

"God speaks in the silence of the heart. Listening is the beginning of prayer."—Mother Teresa

Prayer means different things to different people. For me the point is not about the how to pray, but why to pray.

The purpose of this book is not to be prescriptive, but to encourage Real Estate professionals to consider adding a daily prayer or meditation ritual into their life.

By making meditation as much of a priority as healthy eating and sleeping, I've been empowered beyond my expectations. There is no doubt in my mind that the doors which have opened in my life, whether it be the next client, investor, or grand opportunity, have manifested because of my daily meditation practice. My intention is to share the workings of this with you. I hope that whatever form of religion or spirituality you embrace, becomes more aligned with your career as a result of this awareness. When you incorporate Eat, Sleep, and Pray into your professional life, the Clean Fuel you create is potent.

I have observed that many people keep their forms of religious or spiritual expression isolated from their day to day activities. In my experience, integrating your spiritual practice with all aspects of your life, enables another level of opportunity in your Real Estate career.

It is of course important to cultivate balance. The last thing you want to do is to become over-zealous and to force your practices and beliefs onto others. Instead, allow the newfound regimen to shine through you. I think of this as your *heart light*. In time and with consistent dedication, people may ask you for guidance. But start by being focused on you. This is a great example of Gandhi's famous words, "Be the change you want to see in the world."

I'm confident you will find that a strong religious or spiritual foundation, will add momentum to your Real Estate efforts. The more you are aligned with your purpose, the better prepared you will be when the chaotic world of Real Estate slaps you across the face. And it will.

For many of my early years in the business I relied almost entirely on grit and determination. My mission was to be the hardest worker in the room. I would make it a point to be the first one in and the last one out. At one point I would send emails at 3am followed by a 5am social media post to let everyone know I meant business. Competition is what drove me and I can't dispute that it delivered results. I worked hard, I had a great presence online and, in my community, and as I shared in Chapter One, I became a multimillion dollar producer less than 18 months into the business.

I had always been a spiritual person and felt it was a part of my path, but I hadn't thought about integrating it into my Real Estate life. For a busy broker, free time is a luxury. What with early morning networking events, inspections, Chamber of Commerce meetings and showings in the afternoons, it can feel as though it's impossible to squeeze more into your day. I had no reason to change my game plan. I believed that having a healthy body and getting sufficient sleep was the recipe for success. At this point I was missing the Pray element in my Clean Fuel formula.

But then my performance seemed to have reached its peak and I began to question my methods. I was still closing deals, but the bar wasn't rising. I was no longer gaining momentum. I knew that

I wouldn't hit my next career level unless I evolved. I must have uncovered and practiced every good habit in the Real Estate profession, but suddenly I understood that to achieve more, I needed something greater. Something was missing.

It became evident to me that I needed to feel the connection to a deeper purpose. Taking the time to meditate gave me the ability to hear my true self. I started off gradually and for the first year, five minutes of sitting felt like five hours. The amount of noise in my mind startled me, but I was intrigued enough to continue my practice. As time passed, meditation became easier and the impact on my business was impossible to ignore.

The doors that "never open" opened. The people who "never call" called. The deals that "should not happen" were closed. It wasn't the outside that had changed. It was my inside world. This transformation allowed me to see through others eyes and gave me the ability to truly listen. When others feel you are listening, they feel that you care. It gives them the confidence to trust you with their biggest assets. Trust is essential in the Real Estate business.

A sincere spiritual practice combines extreme stillness, with an infinite supply of energy. There is nothing on this planet that can stop you when you have purpose.

How to Begin

Regardless of your particular spiritual practice, the most important part of this implementation is consistency. You will hear this time and again throughout the book. Pick your time, your place and fully dedicate yourself to it. Turn off the world and let the connection to your higher purpose fuel your day. I suggest that this be done at the start of the day if possible, even before a workout. It's a widely held belief that our minds are clearest and most efficient in the morning. If your schedule prevents an early morning routine, then set the period you can commit to. Even if you have no schedule consistency, your goal can be to carve out the time however you can. I take my commitment seriously and make it a point to practice each day. As you begin to find your flow you will start to see how it affects your mood, energy, focus and clarity. You become less tense, which I believe subconsciously opens doors in all areas.

I believe there is magic in developing your own spiritual practice. Your discipline will pay you back many times over and once established, you won't want to miss it. There have been many times in my life since I began my meditation practice, that complete strangers have approached me and told me I remind them of someone. I have never met these individuals, but we are all more connected than we realize.

[CHAPTER THREE]
FUEL–HEART LIGHT– PURPOSE

Y *ou may have wondered* what I meant by Clean Fuel in the previous chapter. Quite simply, when we burn what I call, Clean Fuel, we are better equipped physically, mentally, and spiritually to pursue our dreams and desires.

This spiritual fuel can be traced back to the beginning of time and is sparked by a higher purpose or an energy at work behind the scenes.

Nothing compares to the light already within us. When we run on clean fuel there's an inner light which radiates out from our hearts, and touches those around us. I call this our Heart Light.

I believe that when we align ourselves with God, whatever that looks like for each of us, we realize that it's not all on us to make everything happen in life. It's a trick of the ego to think we can control everything. It is my experience that cultivating sufficient clean fuel smooths the path to success, both in the Real Estate business and in other endeavors. It allows us to tap into the infinite power beyond our physical, human selves.

Let's explore exactly how Clean Fuel works, so you can more systematically use it in your business and life:

Step 1: Follow Your Heart Light

People call it your intuition, your gut, your inner guidance, your conscience, the angel on your shoulder, and numerous other names. Whichever way you define this sixth sense, once understood and appreciated, it becomes fundamental to living a life of greater ease, joy, and purpose.

In the past, I disregarded my heart light repeatedly, only to discover I had wasted valuable time and in some cases lost a lot of money. A smarter way is to develop this innate superpower so it becomes second nature. Often it takes years of experience and getting your lunch handed to you enough times to wake up to the guidance of your heart light. Waking up to the awareness that you have access to this heart light guidance is crucial. Many people go through life repeating the same mistakes and not learning from them.

"Evolve or die" is a great motto and is relevant when fine tuning your ability to recognize your heart light. As I have gained more life and business experience, my ability to act on the guidance of my heart light has multiplied exponentially.

I'm no longer compelled to touch the fire to know it's hot. I can typically feel my heart light after just a few minutes of speaking with someone. This is particularly helpful in the Real Estate business, where we must deal with so many prospects in order to find the best clients. All of my decisions are now gauged and executed on this feeling.

Many people claim that appearance, wealth, and how you express yourself are the key indicators to who you are. Although this is a great start and not to be ignored, as you move up the ranks of life and business, these superficial things are easily manipulated to throw off the untrained eye. I have known several people who depicted themselves as rich and highly connected, only to find that neither of these things were true. Many recent YouTube entrepreneurs and rising stars are notorious for embellishing their fame and fortune. It's easy for them to rent expensive cars, take pictures on airplanes and claim they want to buy a pro sports team. By learning to tune into your heart light, you'll begin to sense what is true and right for you.

This in no way means your heart light won't jump to a ten on the Richter scale around someone who is successful. The point is that heart light isn't impressed or guided by wealth.

Money has no preference on how it is made. But your heart light does have a preference of who you want to do business with. Begin to pay attention to your heart light. Just because someone is successful, doesn't mean you must partner with them, in the same way it doesn't mean you should not collaborate with someone who hasn't yet attained success. Follow your heart light and always allow it to guide you.

Step 2: Let Go and Say No

Which brings us to the second step. Let go and allow yourself to say no. For many new brokers coming into the Real Estate business, this will be a very difficult task, perhaps even the most challenging. When you're short of cash and feel compelled to make something happen, even the most far-fetched deals will look appealing. But take heed and run if you sense it's not the right move for you. The amount of energy you'll waste and money you'll lose will be worth letting the wrong deal pass you by.

This doesn't mean that you shouldn't do your due diligence and assess the situation in a business-like fashion, but don't waste your time trying to make the wrong thing right only for the money. Move on, or refer the opportunity to someone who may be better suited to it. But if you feel that no one is suited for a particular deal, don't be afraid to politely decline and proceed on to the next opportunity.

This ties into the creation of Clean Fuel. God has a plan and I truly believe would never put us in a position that was not for our betterment . Trust that the best things life has to offer are on their way, when you follow your heart light and act with integrity in line with what you know is right.

Saying no and letting go when necessary, opens up the space for you to recognize your true potential. If you're too busy trying to put together the wrong deal against all of the odds, you'll miss the signpost which is trying to guide you to the perfect next step.

Instead of viewing it as a lost opportunity, think of it as being one step closer to the next right deal.

When our thoughts shift, we access our natural clarity which enables us to notice when the door of opportunity opens. Unless you give yourself permission to say no, let go, and truly mean it, this door will often remain closed. Clinging to the wrong thing will never make it the right thing.

Step 3: Purpose Supplies Clean Fuel

Life without purpose is a treacherous path. If you define your success by the amount of money in your bank account, the car you drive, or other tangible assets, then you're likely to lose steam when the thrill of the prize diminishes.

Many wealthy individuals recognize this because they are able to see for themselves that monetary gain is no guarantee of peace of mind. You may collect a lot of lovely things, but as fun as it may be, possessions do not automatically convert into joy. Peace of mind doesn't come from things, even though our ego tricks us into believing it does. The flashy things in life have a way of hypnotizing us, distracting us from our true self and purpose.

Many high performers get to the top of their respected fields, only to find that nothing awaits them at the summit. They then realize they have missed the point of the journey. Many unknowingly compromise their good health and sacrifice precious time with their loved ones, in their quest to achieve and attain more. You may think, "Well that's easy for you to think. Give me millions of dollars or the kind of opportunities these people have and I bet my endorphin rush would last for years." It's tempting to believe that, but achieving the pinnacle of what society deems as "successful" is but a fleeting moment.

The reality is that most people won't attain this level of worldly success anyway. And it's not because there isn't enough to go around. The universe is abundant, but a lack of clean fuel makes it much more challenging to stay on purpose.

Clean Fuel Formula:
Love + Action = Clean Fuel

Purpose Formula:
Sustainability + Courage = Purpose

Loving what you do no matter what your career, is a reliable recipe for a meaningful life. Whether you are already in Real Estate like me, an author, doctor, or lifeguard, the key to clean fuel starts here. When this love is combined with action, many people define the feeling as a natural high, a flow, or being in the zone. This is the core of Clean Fuel.

When you operate at this level, life slows down, yet results speed up. Doors open and people who can help you, show up as if by magic. This way of living is the path of purpose. When you take this path, the only thing left to get in the way is you. When you understand the formula beyond the simple words, you see that courage is innate.

This way of being is what I define as your Purpose. I believe that each human has access to this flow and no matter what we do and no matter how big or small our actions are, if we act with loving intention then our purpose is instantly fulfilled in each moment.

The destination, although important, pales in comparison to the awareness of living in the now. This perspective on life is a great opportunity to wake up to the power of living your life on purpose.

Resistance Formulas:
Resistance + Action = Unnatural Fuel
Inconsistency + Fear = Off Purpose

Resistance tends to create a life of struggle. To evolve, it's crucial to recognize the mistakes we make and adjust our behavior accordingly. Starting off with anything other than love would be defined as resistance.

Let me be clear, working hard to achieve your real estate or other goals will not always be fun. People frequently confuse a temporary defeat or challenge as a sign to give up. They think for sure they can't be on the right track if it seems difficult. But that's a myth. Sometimes the rainbow lies just over the horizon.

There's no guarantee of achieving a certain result because it's not in our control, which is why following your heart light is the only way to stay in tune with a deeper guidance. This guidance is more reliable than any insecure feelings you experience in the moment. If your heart light indicates the need to change direction, then pay attention. Taking action when you have clarity is the key to achieving more of what you desire.

There is also a lesson in defeat. When you fail, make sure to embrace the lesson and move forward, knowing you will be wiser next time. If you repeatedly make the same mistakes, you are not paying attention and it will eventually cost you.

The difference between those who stay stuck in failure and those who ultimately succeed, is their ability to rapidly learn from their mistakes and adjust their approach. Try new things so that when you fail, it's at something new. This experience will increase your chances of reaching your goals, quicker. The more willing you are to accept your mistakes, the better chance you have of developing your skills. We have no control over outcomes but we have control over our efforts.

The only variable in every situation is you, so always do the best with what you have. Otherwise you will be quick to blame outside forces and never truly find the sustainability required to fulfill your purpose. If you continue to forge the wrong path, fear will derail you. I truly believe that every negative emotion is derived from fear. Some people get angry, others defensive, and many resort to self-pity and denial. But no matter how you react, trace the roots of any negative emotion to its core and it will bring you back to fear. Fear is the killer of dreams and the justification of failure. Many live their entire lives engulfed in fear, only to blame their current predicament on external circumstances. The quickest path to a life without purpose is a life driven by fear.

Clean fuel is the key to a life of purpose and success in Real Estate or any other business for that matter.

[CHAPTER FOUR]
SPEAK THE PART– LOOK THE PART– SMELL THE PART

This chapter carries so much weight, I was tempted to deliver it with a fanfare. Here's why: it is all about you, and what you can do to make an instant and long-lasting impact. Whatever your beliefs and opinions there are a few facts that nobody can wriggle free from. How you sound, how you look, and believe it or not, how you smell, have a direct link to your success.

The information I've laid out for you in this chapter may sound a bit personal, and in part ... uncouth! I'm not calling into question your personality, your character, or your preferences, I am however, laying out the facts to how clients respond to Real Estate brokers who chose not to follow the basics.

You are in business, the Real Estate business: this is not a hobby or a joke side-gig. Clients will always buy and sell properties; they do not need to select you to be their realtor. This chapter will elevate you into the top few percent who understand that these simple basics are crucial for success.

We've all experienced a time when a person stood out from the crowd because of how they spoke, or how they dressed, or simply, how they smelled. And remember, this works both positively and negatively.

I'm going to walk you through the points and drop some of my secrets into your lap. Because, you get one go to make a first impression, more importantly, you only get one chance to make a lasting impression. And, in Real Estate, there is nothing more important.

SPEAK THE PART

"Vocabulary allows us to interpret and express. If you have a limited vocabulary you will also have a limited vision and a limited future."
—Jim Rohn

The ability to communicate clearly, and with a purpose, is the lifeblood of any aspiring Real Estate broker's career. The inability to articulate a clear message lays the rocky groundwork for a challenging path ahead. I want to make the distinction between the confidence to deliver a clear message and those who simply have the gift of gab. I know people who can walk up to a complete stranger and start a conversation like they were their best friend. Although the gift of gab is a great attribute, it's worth remembering it is only the substance of a conversation that truly matters.

Personally, I feel less is more. If you're able to convey your intentions and come to a clear objective, without the need for unnecessary small talk, then you'll soon be on the path to higher levels of success. Successful people I know, all value their time above everything and the last thing they desire is to endure a drawn-out conversation, filled with fluff and repetition. The use of too much small talk in your conversations only highlights your potential lack of knowledge and that you may be trying to pad it with inadequate examples and stories. When it comes to business, stick with the facts and what's important. There is a time and place for everything and you must be able to discern what is appropriate.

Now, with that being said, anyone who knows me, knows I love to communicate (which is a nice way of saying I have a big mouth). An old saying "closed mouths don't get fed" is a truth. That is why having a plethora of communication options is vital in rising to the upper echelon of the Real Estate business. Plus, the only way someone is going to find out what kind of personality you have, and if they are interested in working with you, is to listen to how you communicate. In social settings and networking events there is nothing wrong with being the peacock in the room. But remember, I said peacock, not a blabbering, loud mouth, obnoxious clown.

First impressions are very important and it's better to say less, and be certain, than to over-extend and come across as an amateur. The flow of the conversation must be in rhythm, and both sides should feel as though they are being heard. Because, not being heard is the source of frustration. We've all witnessed that person who sucks all the air out of a room because they are only concerned about getting their point across, rather than listening. Don't let that person be you.

I've discovered, if you listen twice as much as you speak, then most of the things you want to gain from the conversation will come up naturally. Remember the old adage: we have two ears and one mouth for a reason. There is a point to all of this — when your moment comes up to take the floor, then you should do so with impact, intention, and prepare to deliver the "wow factor."

So, how do you leave that kind of impression?

Having a varied and vibrant vocabulary will definitely set you apart from people who constantly churn out the usual tired clichés. An interesting vocabulary also attracts like-minded people. These individuals are typically the ones running the show and will be happy to interact with you once they know you share similarities in the art of expression. It's not to say they would not engage in a polite conversation with you, but doing business may be far less realistic.

People like people who remind them of their own tribe.

The best way to develop an expansive vocabulary is to read. Reading didn't come easily to me. What you read has a profound impact on you. Keep in mind, "Garbage in garbage out". I'm assuming you purchased this book because you want to hone your Real Estate abilities, and be one step closer to your objectives.

We unavoidably judge others by how they speak, and we are being judged by others each time we open our mouths. In that moment of judgement, our level of education, knowledge, and standing in society are being summed up and an opinion is being formed about us in a heartbeat.

Is that fair? – No
Is it a fact? – Yes

I'm not suggesting you should abandon your roots and change your speaking style. You'll find a natural change and seamless improvement will occur simply by reading and listening to high quality material.

Words have power. Think before you use them, and speak from the heart.

"Before you speak let your words pass through three gates: Is it true? Is it necessary? Is it kind?"—Buddha

How does this quote resonate with you?

For most of us we are lucky if we get beyond the instinct to respond, let alone think about multiple things prior to speaking. If we were more thoughtful about what we say, and how we say it, I wholeheartedly believe that people's lives would change drastically. Most people speak to hear themselves talk, not to listen. This is a very limiting position and can make your transaction not only more difficult, but also put you at a strategic disadvantage. Listening to someone speak is only a small component of understanding what they are trying to say. How do they move? What are they looking at? How fast or slow are they speaking? Is there urgency in their tone? These clues can easily be missed because we are too busy worrying about how we are going to respond. Less is more. Trying to fill the silence only detracts from what the moment is trying to teach us.

During a conversation, concentrate as if you were playing a game of chess: What move can you anticipate? How can you add more value? What should be said and, more important, what should not be said? I frequently hear brokers speaking just to hear themselves talk and they end up torpedoing their own opportunities. A golden rule in Real Estate is to speak when a question is asked and only if you know the answer. It's always better to get the facts than to shoot from the hip. Bad information can swing the momentum of deals and make your client lose respect for you. Once that happens, it's very hard to earn it back.

Some of the most influential spiritual leaders have changed the world through their message. From Christ to Buddha, how and what they said had an enormous effect. How did they do that, how did they create such great impact? Maybe the better question is why? Remember, success is measured in inches, in tiny details, and achieved behind the scenes when nobody sees. The most dynamic messages have come from a place of truth, a place of knowing, and from a clear — why.

66

First impressions are very important and it's better to say less and be certain, than to over-extend and come across as an amateur.

99

Being a master of your craft must come from a deeper connection. The Clean Fuel analogy really works here as well. When you have purpose and you surrender to it no matter the outcome, you can't lose. Each step, whether good, bad, easy, or hard is just another mini victory as you edge closer to mastery. Mastery is when all of God's tools are realized and focused on your desires. Those recognized as master communicators have changed the world. With that in mind, imagine what it could do for your Real Estate career. Your communication skills must be one of the key foundations of your business. There is no way around this and there are no short cuts. If you fail to make this a priority, then you will not excel.

LOOK THE PART

"You cannot climb the ladder of success dressed in a costume of failure."—Zig Ziglar

One thing is for sure: how a person dresses can be a great indicator of how their performance will play out as a Real Estate broker. You can argue about this all day long, but in the end the fact remains, how an individual dresses can be tied to their level of success. Dressing appropriately for the occasion is important too. However, I don't believe this should be used as an excuse to dress down, or beneath your usual standards. Personally, I never sacrifice my dress-code in order to make someone feel more comfortable. Your clothing cannot conceal the real you, and ultimately your true identity pushes through to the forefront. Clothing is an extension of the individual. Your fashion sense speaks volumes about you and it allows you to stake your claim on what you represent.

Dressing well is generally a selfish activity. Its purpose is to make you feel more confident. Dressing well gives you an edge and when you take this approach, you'll start to see the effects in your business immediately. You'll command respect and ooze authority, and in the

Real Estate business this is true currency. Remember, you're in charge of one of the most important and expensive assets in a person's life. Therefore, at the very least, you must show that you care enough to iron your shirt or blouse and polish your shoes. Opportunities don't wait for anyone, so always being prepared, even when you don't expect things to happen, is crucial if you want to reach great heights in Real Estate.

When I was working in a large office with several hundred brokers, I was baffled by some of their getups. Everything from sweatpants, ball caps, slippers, and sports jerseys. On one occasion, I heard a broker declare he was heading to a closing and he was wearing shorts and a tank top. (If we were in Hawaii this would be a bit more understandable, but we weren't …)

I don't expect everyone to be dressed in a three-piece suit or look like they walked out of a fashion catalogue all the time. Nice clothes can be very expensive and it takes time to build a good wardrobe. However, I do feel being conscientious about fashion to some degree is important and having a unique twist in one's style can also be a great branding strategy. One great example is wearing a bow-tie or suspenders; both are great alternatives to the norm, not overly expensive and are also potential conversation starters. Thinking about how to encourage others to engage with you as much as possible is a key component of the Real Estate business. Small details can go a long way and make the difference when it comes to attracting a new client. More important, it gives someone a reason to remember you. To stand out in a busy market place is paramount to building a successful business.

Unfortunately, in Real Estate, people tend to forget about brokers, and it's not uncommon that the next time they see you, they let you know they are about to buy or sell a property. Leaving a potential client with a great impression is vital, but being the "bow-tie guy" or the "suspender guy" who gets the call when it's time to buy, is infinitely better than having your business card lost in the shuffle. Just some food for thought, but it's worked wonders for me, and has been one of my secrets to success.

Dressing well is not for everyone, I understand that, and if you're the type who doesn't care about clothing and are looking for the easiest way to get through this chapter, the most effective route would be to stick with classic colors. Black, grey, white, and navy blue are safe and are always in style, and can be enhanced with virtually any color to add some pop. The slightest adjustment can help you stand out from the crowd.

Appearance has power. Be conscious of the occasion and what you want to project.

"Clothes make the man. Naked people have little or no influence on society."—Mark Twain

Jesus and Buddha had their robes and sandals. Although they didn't wear the latest Ferragamo boots and Gucci belts, we never hear anything unusual or inconsistent about their attire. The point is this: consistency goes a long way and being presentable when you engage in the Real Estate world really does matter.

I'm not a big brand name guy. When a designer's goal is to plaster their trademark all over the merchandise it becomes more about status and less about quality. This does not mean I do not own expensive clothes, or accessories, however it's rare that style will trump comfort and functionality. A standout piece of clothing is a great strategy when you find yourself in an ocean of white shits and blue blazers. Being memorable is key, but less is more and continuity will always work in your favor.

When I look at clothes, I think about how each piece will harmonize with my personality and my Real Estate wardrobe. How seriously you take your style is how seriously the market will take you. Clothing can be considered an art. The artist is the designer. The average designer, versus the above average designer is apparent. Like Michelangelo when he created his masterpieces, a passionate and creative designer or artist can turn heads. There is a fine line between art and fashion and how you put it together is personal preference.

SMELL THE PART

"Of the five senses, smell is the one with the best memory."—Rebecca McClanahan

This final focus holds a prized place in my beliefs. Smelling the part means exactly what it states. If you smell like an old sock you'll be remembered as the smelly person.

It takes time to learn fresh, vibrant vocabulary and it requires investment to build an impressive wardrobe. I get it, I've been there. But there should be few, if any, excuses for anyone to smell bad. As a child most of us can remember certain smells that would fill us with joy and excitement. Maybe it was Mom's cookies, Dad's BBQ, or Grandma's fresh bread from the oven. Ah, I can smell it now. How about a certain place you visited: a beach with the evocative smell of the sea, a deep breath of fresh forest air, or the busy streets of a city that clogged your nose with the stench of car exhaust, trash, and smog. Either way, it's the smell that rushes you back to that place in a vivid fashion.

My point is this: the sense of smell is a compelling way to impact your interactions with others for far less effort and cost than reading books or wearing the newest fashion trend. Now, I know what you are thinking: Alex, you must be mad, are you telling me that if I smell good then my business will improve? I promise you, once you focus on this, and give it a go, this tiny adjustment will turn heads. Not just metaphorically, but literally.

I must admit, I am an extremist when it comes to these three topics, and can attest that each one, when pushed to the extreme, has always rewarded me with significant returns. My collection of colognes today would rival a small department store, but the right scent can be a conversation starter. Countless times, a discussion has opened up because of a wonderful fragrance. And it's worth remembering, that initiating a conversation is very difficult for most people. Therefore, every opportunity, and every chance should be taken to prompt a conversation. When you look at it from this perspective, you'll see that you're genuinely helping the other person to engage and converse with you.

The type and style of scent you choose is personal and must be selected with care. To you it may smell appealing, but to someone else it might trigger an opposite reaction. Keep in mind, a little goes a long way. Three good sprays of a scent do the trick. Oil based scents tend to last longer because they won't dissipate as fast as alcohol based scents and will stay on your clothes and skin for longer. The easiest way to know if your scent is working for you is simple: count how many people tell you how good you smell. Smelling good may seem trivial, but in my experience, it's a detail that adds another layer in your Real Estate arsenal. If you're just not big on scents or have allergic reactions, then a simple fabric softener or lotion is a good option. Smelling good is an intentional approach that if applied with care and awareness, can help you leave a lasting impression. How you leave it, is completely up to you.

Smell has power. Be mindful that smell is the invisible influencer.
"Nothing is more memorable than a smell. One scent can be unexpected, momentary and fleeting, yet conjure up a childhood summer beside a lake in the mountains."—Diane Ackerman
Choose your perfumes with care. Make sure they complement

your skin because fragrances smell different from person to person. If variety is important to you, alcohol-based perfumes will be your best bet. If you prefer natural, organic products, you'll probably gravitate towards oil-based scents.

Putting it Together with Heart Light

How you talk, how you look, and how you smell share a common thread. These elements tie in with your higher source, and how much love and respect you have for yourself. Quite simply, when you know you're loved and cannot fail, you'll never be fearful of growth. Do not fail to learn that a willingness to grow is vital and that an unwillingness to grow will become a hinderance which will hold you back as you attempt to climb the ladder of success. People at the top are there because they never stopped learning, never stopped achieving, and continue to do whatever is necessary to keep moving forward.

Ultimately, your goal is to feel good about yourself. Why would you not dress, speak and smell as well as you possibly can? After all, the Real Estate business exchanges one of the most expensive and important items a person will ever buy in their lifetime.

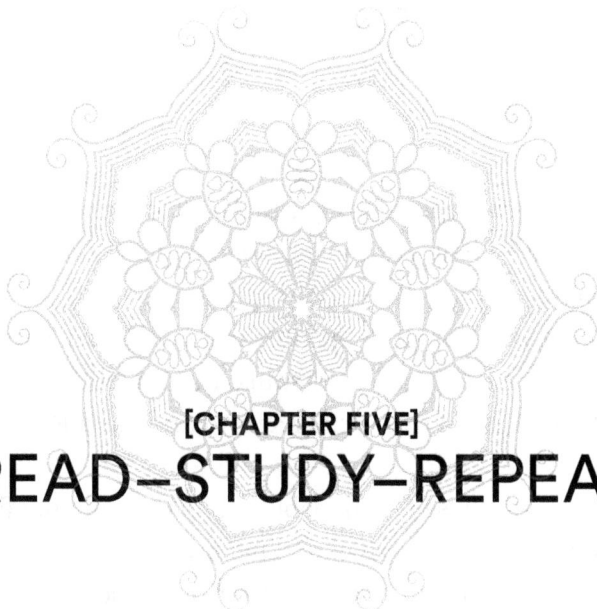

[CHAPTER FIVE]
READ–STUDY–REPEAT

*The more that you read, the more things you will know.
The more that you learn, the more places you'll go.*
—Dr. Seuss

This chapter is dedicated to self-education through reading because it is such an important topic for anyone who desires to achieve outstanding results. My goal is to encourage you to develop self-education as a habit.

For most of my life I avoided reading, so don't be alarmed if you're not yet much of a reader. At school, I read only what was required of me, and even then, if given the choice between reading a whole book or study notes, I would choose the cheat sheet. Up until my mid-twenties, I was obsessed with the latest sports statistics and video games. I had no interest in books. Much of my time and energy was spent in debating with my friends about the performance of prominent players and who was being sought by which team. After a day at work I would slump on the couch, throw on some Madden or Call of Duty, and before I knew it, three or four hours had passed. Then I would head to bed and wake up to start the process all over again the next morning. During the weekends, my ritual was to wake up late, eat, and then play a couple of hours of games, stopping just in time to turn on the afternoon marathon of the current sports season.

I now kick myself for all of the time that could have been allocated to educating myself and honing my skills. I could tell you every athlete's stat, but none of this furthered my career as a Real Estate professional.

I continued with these questionable habits well into my fifth year in the business. I was a top producer and there were no complaints from my broker, but I was always a step or two behind the leading brokers. The phrase "Hard work beats talent, when talent doesn't work" rings true. I came to the realization that unless I began to apply myself more seriously, I wouldn't fulfil my potential.

Reading about the technical elements of business was a challenge for me. I wasn't motivated to learn about contracts and Real Estate law because it's such a dry subject. When I started out, I cared more about getting someone under contract, than I did about the contract terms. My broker understood my attitude and I was fortunate to benefit from his expertise and guidance throughout each deal. I would probably have run into some serious problems without his mentorship.

Many other brokers are technically savvy, but don't have the personal touch that is so critical for dealing with people. We are all different but we can all benefit from deepening our knowledge and developing our skills.

For some it makes sense to continue formal education, but for most professionals already working a full-time job or running a business, reading is an inexpensive and simple way to develop yourself. If you're not much of a reader, I recommend that you begin by reading books that interest you. Forcing yourself to read a book which doesn't appeal to you, will make it more difficult to embrace reading as a daily practice. It's easier to develop the habit of reading consistently when you're enthusiastic about your book choice. You can start with smaller books, of which there is no shortage in the business and personal development genres. Authors know that professionals are short on time, so a great book doesn't have to be a long book. Just as if you were trying to get fit, you wouldn't run a marathon as your first event.

It requires discipline to make yourself read a book that doesn't grab your attention immediately, and trying to pull yourself through a long book which doesn't interest you, won't set you up for success. This is not to say you won't benefit from reading books you find dull. I've read dozens of authors whose writing didn't appeal to me. But reading them was still worth my time. I always extract at least one jewel from every book. You may even read only particular sections of some books because you want specialized information and the entire book isn't relevant. It all depends on the genre and topic.

> 66
>
> **Authors know that professionals are short on time, so a great book doesn't have to be a long book.**
>
> 99

As you immerse yourself in reading, you'll also discover books you don't want to put down, and can't wait to get back to reading. As a result, your world begins to transform from the inside-out. You experience "aha" moments which spark a new understanding of the subject matter.

You may wonder how you'll know which books to read. It can be overwhelming when faced with thousands of books to choose from. In my experience, the best way to find great books is to follow the authors who have already inspired you through their books. You will start to see a pattern in the books you read and the people who write them. When you're interested in someone's business or opinions, you'll usually be interested in the topic of the books they read. Also, once you become a dedicated reader, you'll naturally talk to others about the books you're reading and, in this way, you'll receive word of mouth recommendations.

From a networking point of view, it's an ice-breaker to be able to talk to prospects about the latest books you've read on a topic that interests them. People will be impressed and see you as an informed individual. Just like being a published author establishes your authority, reading books deepens your expertise on your topic and broadens your perspective on life. It's beneficial to have the confidence to discuss anything with anybody, even if you're not an expert on the topic. This is one of the ways you develop rapport with potential clients and networking partners.

I recommend that you maintain balance in your reading selection. Real Estate professionals are considered to be entrepreneurs. We determine our own hours and we get paid on results. Keeping abreast of trends and projections is critical if you want to be at the top of the field.

But, to develop a broad range of knowledge, I encourage you to read on a diverse range of subjects such as psychology, self-help, communication, history, autobiographies, and spiritual texts. Personally, I like to read at least one Real Estate book per quarter, to keep up with current industry developments. At the end of this chapter I will include my top ten recommended books to give you some new ideas. Also, if you've been trying to read more and not succeeding, the chances are you've got a pile of books waiting for your attention at home.

As I read more, my inner world expanded and my perspective on life broadened so that I was better equipped to handle whatever was thrown at me.

The best way I can describe this transformation is that my mind became efficient. With this new clarity, solutions began to click into place, I was more intuitive about what people wanted and I could anticipate problems in time to course correct. My awareness had deepened and I was in touch with a deeper part of myself. Until then I had no idea this amazing ability existed. It was like suddenly discovering I had a superpower. At this point I knew I was hooked. Reading stopped being a discipline and became a joy. I believe this transformation occurred as a result of the combination of my consistent spiritual practice and my immersion in personal development. As a former athlete and body builder, I was familiar with the beauty of working out to improve my body. The more frequently you train, the faster the results. I took this same approach to reading and I soon noticed the impact, both in my state of mind and in my life. I went from reading one book a month, to two, to four and now I try to get through at least eight to ten a month. I heard that Warren Buffet reads six hundred to one thousand pages a day which is the equivalent of two or three books. Other legends like Bill Gates, Elon Musk and Oprah are also avid readers. All of these people are leaders in their fields and have changed the world in some way.

The point is that you may be born with a great mind but even great minds require cultivating. Success typically doesn't happen overnight, it takes time and dedication. Twenty years is a magic number when we talk about anyone noteworthy hitting their ultimate goals. In the process of pursuing success, they tend to influence their industries. This is not a coincidence, being focused on learning what's relevant to achieve your goals, makes evolution inevitable. But the trick is to give yourself the best environment for success to occur.

As we are all currently using our twenty-four hours each day, unless you already have allocated time for personal development, reading will need to become a new priority.

Here are my top tips to carve out the time to either start or to scale up your reading routine.

- Cancel cable TV
- Limit mobile and all device usage
- Block out time in your schedule each day
- Incorporate reading into other activities by listening to audio books

TV has become engrained in our culture. So much so that it's not uncommon to hear people talk about binge watching their favorite shows for hours at a time. Daily discussions about the latest events and what's in store for the next episodes are common. I'm not opposed to the occasional movie, but I think the amount of time wasted watching TV is appalling. According to a Nielson report, adults in the United States watch approximately five hours of television per day. And that's not taking into account how much time spent on social media.

Based on these numbers you would think people were getting paid to watch television, since the amount of time is almost equivalent to a full-time job. The moment I ended my addiction to cable TV and decided to invest that time into reading was a defining one. It took a lot of discipline and commitment because I loved watching TV. Of course, it's different for every person and may not be an issue for you at all. Perhaps you have other daily habits which consume a lot of your day which you can consider substituting for reading time. When you're ready for change, change can happen effortlessly. It doesn't always have to be hard, but quitting TV was a challenge for me. Don't be discouraged if changing a long-standing habit takes effort. You'll look back and wonder why you didn't do it earlier because the pay-off is so rewarding.

From a social perspective, it can be challenging to relate to others who follow the current popular shows and want to chat about them. The biggest shock for me was how quiet my house was without the incessant background noise of the TV. I began to notice what was going on in my mind. It was like a veil had been lifted because I had innocently used TV as a mind-numbing distraction. Although I didn't watch five hours of television per day, it was not uncommon for me to be hooked on regular sports events. Most games, such as basketball, football or fights, typically last a couple of hours.

It wasn't easy to trade in my remote, for a book, but it was worth it. Watching most television shows, unless they're educational, takes minimal brain exertion which is why it's such a popular pastime. Reading takes more energy, especially when you're reading educational material. The mind is in some ways like a muscle and it takes practice to get into the habit of reading. Initially, my attention wandered and I found it difficult to absorb information. I would take breaks, walk around the house and grab a glass of water or a snack. I wasn't used to focusing in that way. The distraction of my phone made it more challenging to concentrate. I think it took two years of daily reading to engrain the new "reading grooves" in my brain. My advice is to start with at least twenty minutes reading each day. As you build the habit you'll hopefully enjoy reading and will also begin to read faster and be able to extract relevant points with greater ease. Personally, I don't read educational or self-improvement books before trying to sleep. I like to give my mind at least an hour to unwind. Trying to cram information into your brain when you're tired isn't productive because it's unlikely you'll retain it anyway. I don't like to stimulate my mind too much at bedtime because I begin over-thinking and then struggle to relax enough to fall sleep. We all need to find the routine which suits each of us.

According to eMarketer, adults in the United States spent an average of three hours and thirty-five minutes per day on mobile devices in 2018 and mobile is predicted to surpass TV as the medium attracting the most minutes in the US.

Real Estate professionals do need to keep themselves informed of what's going on in their industry so I'm not saying to turn everything off. But it's a fine line between studying the latest trends and scrolling aimlessly through social media which many people do.

Video games were also a huge addiction for me. It was a habit I needed to end in order to up-level my business game. Growing up in the era of Nintendo and owning many consoles up until my mid-twenties, the video game evolution was a big part of my life. The shift from intensive video game playing to reading, didn't happen overnight but I quickly saw a vast difference in my ability to focus. An addiction to playing video games consumes hours or even days of your life. The appeal of popular games is their ability to immerse the gamer into a different world. It's amazing how quickly two hours flies by and before you know it you have peeled off half of your day or squandered a full night's sleep. The result is that not only do you spend your time playing, but you also set yourself up for an unproductive day because you haven't slept enough.

These were the habits which distracted me and stopped me from reaching my potential. We all have our weaknesses so I encourage you to identify yours. Awareness is the first step to change. Begin to adjust your schedule to make more space in your life and your mind so you can focus on what you want to achieve.

Listening to audio books when you're doing repetitive type activities such as working out, cooking or cleaning is a great way to consume more books and make the most of your time. You can also turn your car into a classroom or listen to audiobooks whilst commuting.

Here is my recommended top ten book list:

- *Siddhartha* by Hermann Hesse
- *A Course in Miracles* by Helen Schucman
- *Illusions: The Adventures of a Reluctant Messiah* by Richard Bach
- *The Alchemist* by Paulo Coelho
- *The Untethered Soul* by Michael Singer
- *Man's Search for Meaning* by Viktor E Frankl
- *The Laws of Success* by Napoleon Hill
- *Tribe of Mentors* by Tim Ferriss
- *Principles* by Ray Dalio
- *The Laws of Human Nature* by Robert Greene

(CLOCKWISE FROM LEFT)

With D-Bo!,
Pep's hardware
(SuperBowl XLV),
With Brandon
Burton

(CLOCKWISE FROM LEFT)

With Mike Morgan in Cancun (SuperBowl XLVII Champ), With Mike Miller in Miami (after 2012 Championship win), with Sly and Rojo in Utah!, with crew at Life Beyond Football NFL Retreat

(CLOCKWISE FROM LEFT)

With Malik Jackson (SuperBowl 50 Champ), Ant's hardware (SuperBowl XLIII Champ), with Anthony Madison, with Mayweather Sr. in Vegas at TMT Gym

(CLOCKWISE FROM LEFT)

With Rob Garcia (legendary strength coach), with Sly!, with Ant and Pep in Cancun

(CLOCKWISE FROM LEFT)

Red carpet event in Hollywood, with Sly before charity event, 2nd TV interview for Berkshire Hathaway acquisition

(CLOCKWISE FROM LEFT)

Berkshire Hathaway Acquisition interview with Greg Frost Sr., with Greg Frost Sr., with Mike and friends at charity event

(ON OPPOSITE PAGE)

Me and Sly!

(CLOCKWISE FROM LEFT)

With my mentor, Mike's hardware (2012 NBA Championship) with Ryan and Mike Miller—Class acts!

"

In the end, when your purpose is clear,
life tends to give you more than you could ever ask for.

"

[CHAPTER SIX]
BREAKING THE PATTERN–
HABITS–GOALS

reaking a pattern sets us free. And, breaking free is a major component in our journey towards a successful career in Real Estate.

A pattern is a subconscious set of actions that we execute without thought, over and over again. Think about it, we get in our car and go through a set of moves, without conscious thought, and find ourselves driving down streets day in, and day out. We need patterns, we rely on patterns, and we trust patterns to get us through repetitive actions. Our brains are hard-wired to get on with these repetitions while we get on with our lives.

It's worth remembering that patterns are neither good nor bad, positive or negative. It is up to us to put the meaning on each of our patterns and decide for ourselves if they help us or hinder us. The true danger lies in the fact that a pattern can manifest itself as a warm comfort blanket of certainty. And that, if we were to break free from it, we might just be left out in the cold. But (and this is the big one), in order for us to grow, we must break free and break through any pattern, which halts our continued success.

Breaking the pattern is crucial in anything in life if you have topped out, hit a ceiling, or worse, declined or failed. Too many people drift aimlessly into patterns that lead to repetitive cycles and dead ends. And yet, they prefer this than the short-term difficulties that dynamic change brings about.

Patterns form habits and there is no exception in the Real Estate business. These habits can drive us forward, or hold us back from achieving the success we crave in life. It's a commonly held view that breaking an old habit such as smoking, drinking, or poor eating, is far harder than establishing a new life affirming practice. The same is true for breaking the pattern of a toxic relationship, or to create the urge to self-educate and learn new skills.

Most of us can resonate with the pain of trying to generate the habit to exercise. Because the habit of not exercising is a human mouse trap. A trap that catches so many people who believe the process of change, is more painful than remaining where they are. It's strange, but there is familiarity and comfort in staying in our present state, even if it is a painful place to be.

You probably know someone who appears unwilling to get off their butt and hit the gym, or get out of a dreadful relationship they are constantly complaining about. From the point of view of business, it is all too common for people to get into a routine and stick to it rather than challenge themselves to change their approach and tactics. I quickly understood that once I decided to change myself, by changing my patterns and habits, life would open up in completely different ways and more opportunities would present themselves. But most importantly, I recognized that I had to want to change, in order for me to break free from my self-imposed shackles.

And there's the clue: we truly and wholeheartedly have to want to change. We have to want to replace the old way with the new, and know that in doing so, an improved way can emerge. To break any pattern, you have to make the conscious decision to do something different in "normal" moments and be prepared to embed it. Those moments are when you are typically on autopilot. If your performance is not where you want it to be, then it is necessary to break the form of what you've been doing and try a different direction.

Breaking a pattern comes from consistent change. Not a day or a week of change, but in my experience, at least ninety days of change. This is a more realistic timeline to evoke any kind of genuine pattern interruption. I recorded real and positive differences in my Real Estate business when I spent three months or more switching my method of operation. If you desire a boost in your results then you'll have to dedicate time for change to occur.

Attending one networking event, or making one cold call, or spending one day posting on social media, are all one-off stabs at change, which are unlikely to impact your Real Estate business for the long term. Similarly, eating well, or going to bed early to recharge your batteries for a few days, is not sufficient to see positive results in your energy levels. The only proven way to manifest change is when it becomes a habit. Until then, it's just a fad.

Setting a series of small goals over a prolonged period of time is a tried and tested method to transition into a bigger breakthrough. Let's say your goal is to meditate for an hour a day — try starting with five minutes a day for two weeks, then ten minutes, and then twenty minutes, until you build up to an hour a day. Maybe your goal is to get up at 5am each morning and you currently get up at 7am. Break it down into smaller intervals — move your wake-up time up by fifteen- or thirty-minutes every couple of weeks. Within a few months you'll be awake at 5am without feeling exhausted.

What if you want to network more each week? I suggest you join a paid group so you make it a priority to attend events and you'll see a return on your investment. The examples are endless. To create a new habit with small, consistent changes works, be patient and committed and you will see a breakthrough. Even your wardrobe can apply: buy and wear one new item of clothing a month and you'll see radical new options and changes in your patterns of dress attire.

We are all creatures of habit and we get used to the same things out of convenience. Try doing things differently in your day-to-day routine. Try driving a different way to work, turn left not right, order tea instead of coffee, take a shower in a different bathroom in your house, wear something you haven't worn in months, go to a restaurant you've never been to before, read a different genre of book, listen to new music, brush your teeth or eat dinner with your non-dominant hand. I know it sounds crazy, but it works, you'll nudge your routines off kilter to find a new track. I do these mind tricks all the time to shock my brain out of cruise control mode.

> **Ask yourself why you do what you do, keep asking, and keep seeking a better way.**

Travel is an unbelievable way to break the pattern. Even if you can only get away to the nearest town over the hill for a long weekend, do it. Traveling is a key way to make changes in your daily patterns. Here's why: "creative thought and opportunities come from a mind that is in uncharted territory". I can't stress highly enough the energy that I've received from this concept. It has given me a priceless bounty of fresh new ideas. Remember, it's not the scenery that's better, although the beaches in Phuket are stunning. It's the peace of mind and the pattern interruption that traveling gives you which prompts your creative brain to come alive. Your mind begins to fire off ideas and creative thought at a pace you may never have witnessed before.

I often hear people say, "nothing changed, it didn't work," or "I'm in the same old place." I then find they didn't record their starting point, so they didn't record the small, incremental improvements, and they didn't study the gauges to stay on track. The rule is: keep a journal and record your patterns. Because you are less likely to change what you can't measure. Do it, even if it's a simple checking system that shows how many times you slipped up on your diet, or how you're increasing your daily meditation minutes. Recording your journey is your personal barometer to break your patterns and implement your goals.

Ask a better question: question everything! Ask yourself why you do what you do, keep asking, and keep seeking a better way. Often, the key to breaking a barrier and changing a pattern is as simple as asking a few more questions. We are way too easily seduced with the status quo. Asking ourselves why we do what we do, really helps open up new opportunities for us.

Any Real Estate professional or entrepreneur knows how easy it is to bury yourself in your work and avoid making time for you, some alone time, some peaceful time. Don't wait until your battery is almost dead before you realize you need to break out. Affording yourself the same habit of travel and leisure is just as critical as eating, sleeping and working out.

Make alone time for yourself.

Only a quiet mind can pinpoint the most stubborn and deep-rooted patterns. Subconsciously, we want to stay busy in order to not think or feel. We will do anything to avoid thinking or feeling, and within my entrepreneur circles it's an epidemic. Take time each day to understand the genuine reason that lies behind an unhealthy pattern. This is a major step in locating the root cause. The psychological component is the most crucial part in breaking any pattern. If you can't understand the why, the how never fully works. The "why" you do something is vastly more valuable to understand than the "how" you do something.

In life, and in Real Estate, our inability to change what's in our mind prevents the complete acceptance needed to create a new pattern. Many discover the reason a diet or exercise regimen doesn't work is not because of anything physical, but because of unresolved issues that have yet to be addressed. This can have a huge impact on their life and career. In Real Estate, your attitude and what you emote is crucial to your success. If you have internal roadblocks, and unresolved issues, they will always make the journey harder. Make time for you, let your quiet mind seek out the internal unresolved issues, deal with them, and break the pattern.

Life balance and better health can often lead to a pattern interrupt. However, it's not uncommon to believe that more of something must be better. More money, more success, more cars, more clothes. And, that working and pushing more, until the results appear, is vital to break a pattern and achieve your goals. This is not only a false narrative, but a recipe for disaster.

Exhaustion is real and can have severe life altering consequences. The reason the mantra of this chapter is "Break the Pattern" is due to some very real personal experiences. One in particular I would have preferred to avoid, but unfortunately, only when we push to our limits, do we know how to learn from them. Hopefully, in reading this you can take away how important breaking bad habits really is and not wait until you learn the hard way, like I did.

At this point you may take it that I'm a type A, militant person. To give you some perspective, I have eaten the same breakfast for the past decade. Egg whites with salsa, a cup of coffee, a cup of freshly squeezed juice, and two pieces of Ezekiel toast with almond butter and ghee (a type of butter). I have my clothes ready for the next day, I have my notes and work routine outlined each evening for each day, I'm at the gym no less than five days a week (and have not missed that in over twenty years!), and I have meditated every day for over fifteen years. Needless to say, I have created quite a few habits in my life. To this day I still partake in all of these processes in my day-to-day living, they have brought me success, joy, and peace of mind. Discipline and structure in a world of chaos, enables things to keep moving, when in most cases, for most people, life tends to just stop.

With that said, the opposite can become true when your habits consume you. Tunnel vision and obsession can damage the very foundation you are trying to create. It's one thing to work hard, it's another to be destructive. For me, only when I ended up hurting the ones I loved, because I was so dead set in my ways and experiencing serious medical issues, did I realize just how crucial changing patterns and accepting change truly is.

At times my fixation with habits would not allow me to relax. An example, was being invited to a simple lunch meeting by a person I love and care for. In my mind I had my routine: chicken salad and an iced tea with one sweetener. The invite was to a new restaurant which offered Cajun seafood in a plastic bag that was vigorously shaken at our table. You would then proceed to put on your bib, open the bag and pull out the different kinds of offerings: crab legs, corn on the cob, shrimp. Sounds fun, right? Well, in my mind it sounded horrific! Too messy, too much going on, too different. The pattern, for me was off, way off.

Reading this may sound comical, and I would agree. However, the negative repercussions of my fixed pattern came full circle. While resentfully eating lunch, an oily, plump, antenna bearing shrimp head, flew out of my plastic bag, bypassed my bib, and landed squarely in the middle of my silk tie. And that, was all that was needed for me to explode. Verbally taking it out on someone who's only intention was to show this ex-chef, a great new place to eat, was completely unjustified. In that moment, it highlighted to me how being so rigid was not a source of strength. In fact it was nothing more than my feeble attempt at control.

The more serious experience was during a very big and complex 1031 exchange. The stakes were high, it was a 10-million-dollar deal and one that I would be double-ending (representing both buyer and seller and essentially doubling my commission). From the start, the deal was choppy. Each moment the lender would require more paperwork, and extension after extension. In a 1031 deal, time is not on your side. Once a property is identified, the buyer only has a set period of time before it expires. Our closing date was sixty days out (a standard timeline in this type of deal), but ended up being pushed out to almost five months. If that wasn't enough, during the last couple of weeks prior to closing, one of the apartments was intentionally set on fire. There are no words that can quantify what that did to me. Months of work, hours of calls and endless emails, were all literally up in smoke. There was no way a lender would ever give a loan for a building that was half burned down. To say I was defeated, would be putting it mildly. But somehow, we found a way. The buyer was getting such a great deal that he ended up paying cash and bypassed the banks. Wow! We made it through, the deal closed, everyone was happy.

But at what cost?

Five months of anything with this heightened stress level will take its toll, and for me it was to the tune of a full system shut down, and excessive hair loss. I was so exhausted from the deal that I stayed at home for a couple weeks to recoup. Fortunately, I also had a trip planned a few days later and retreated to the beach for the next twenty-five days.

> 66
>
> ## Changes should be tackled methodically and mindfully.
>
> 99

My body is still recovering, and anytime I encounter higher than normal stress situations, I can feel it. I visited a dermatologist, for my hair loss, and I was diagnosed with alopecia (a common side effect from excessive stress). After about eight months and several steroid injections to my skull, I'm now much better. I'm happy to report my hair has grown back in its entirety.

So, what did I learn? Any habit can be bad if you don't step back and make sure it's in balance with your life. The need to change it, when you see any signs of negativity, are a must. Do I regret anything? Yes. Sacrificing the people you love is not worth any sort of goal. Even if it's unintentional, you need to be more aware of your actions. Furthermore, hurting yourself is never a sacrifice worth enduring. I was lucky. In many cases, I know people who didn't recover and their relationships were not salvageable.

Changes should be tackled methodically and mindfully. You'll soon hit roadblocks if you think you can start working out five days a week for two hours a day, especially if you haven't been to a gym in ten years. You can't suddenly start waking up at 5am and going to bed at 2am and not expect to burn out, and yet, I see this happening all the time. Breaking a pattern doesn't mean forcefully changing what you do. It means testing new methods and ideas gradually, and most importantly, consistently over time. This approach doesn't negate hard work and long hours. But, it does mean that when you choose this path, all the segments in your life will balance out to support the whole picture.

And here's a fascinating yet inconvenient truth: a negative pattern can also and easily be developed by attempting to break an old pattern. So, take heed in your approach. Just because you are trying to change things up, it doesn't mean they are always for the best. Following new trends blindly without doing your due diligence, is just as harmful as staying in a bad pattern. So much time can be wasted on the "next best thing" only to find out it wasn't right for you. This is not to say you shouldn't be open to embrace new ideas, however, make sure the ideas are in line with your long-term goals. It takes a lot of saying no; and saying no to what you already know is hard, especially when you don't want to. When you find the balance between the tested and true, and the new and improved, you know you're on your way to breaking a pattern.

These are the steps that have helped me become efficient at change:

1. Identify the pattern you want to change.
2. Determine why you "want" to change.
3. Replace the old pattern with a new one.
4. Record your incremental changes.
5. Let time pass (at least 90 days) to create the new pattern.

Guarding yourself against slipping into a life of complacency, and guarding yourself against running a Real Estate business of mediocrity, requires a self-imposed, full-time sense of responsibility. Real Estate requires a mindset that allows you to seek out failing methods, and then break through habits and barriers that do not serve you or your business. In order to succeed in Real Estate, you have to actively track down habits that don't work for you and replace it with a positive new pattern forming habit.

Putting it Together with Heart Light

Patterns give us comfort. Familiarity, consistency, and the anticipation of anything noteworthy in life, is what we live for. In business, patterns have made entrepreneurs very successful. People go back to establishments like Starbucks because they know what they can expect.

Monks, priests, and those who have embarked on a spiritual life typically partake in daily rituals or patterns. From meditation, prayer, chanting, to religious dancing, they are all done with very similar consistency and intent. The beauty in patterns can be seen throughout time and with a track record with this kind of success and clarity. It's no wonder humans began to embrace them in other variations. Patterns and habits are ingrained in our DNA. Knowing that, hopefully makes it clearer on exactly what you are up against when you embark on changing an old habit or embracing a new one.

When you embark upon an attempt to break any pattern, it takes diligence, patience, consistency and resolve. The subconscious mind is always at work and so has far more advantages. It's always working, 24 hours a day. That's why it's so crucial to stay the course and be consistent.

Embracing your faith and bringing your heart light into play can also be a great option. Having a why, gives us all a stronger purpose and much more leverage when you begin to revert back to old habits. Knowing inside when you "should" or "shouldn't" exercise a habit can only magnify when you embrace your heart light and have the courage to follow it. It can be a lonely path, but anything great is never easy and is worth it when you reach the mountain top.

[CHAPTER SEVEN]
MARKETING– CONNECTION–SERVICE

> 66
>
> Half the money I spend on advertising is wasted;
> the trouble is, I don't know which half.
> **—John Wanamaker**
>
> 99

n this chapter I want to talk about the importance of marketing and give you some direction for this essential component of building a successful Real Estate business.

Marketing isn't an exact science and for that reason it can be confusing. Consistency is the key to successful marketing. You can't know what's working if you only dabble in a number of methods, but don't stick with them. This is challenging because marketing costs both time and money. Even if you don't invest in advertising when you start out, using free methods typically requires a lot of time. Every moment spent marketing is time away from your other business activities, which in turn costs money.

If you pick a marketing method today, you've got to do it for long enough to give it a chance to work for you.

Keep your chosen activity running for sufficient time so you can track whether it converts into sales. Only from that position can you adjust your marketing accordingly.

It's a tough gauge because seeing it through requires investment. It's easy to lose your confidence halfway through a marketing campaign, especially if you already have reservations about investing your marketing dollars.

If you were to diet for only two weeks, you'd obviously have less chance of achieving your desired results. Most people need to be consistent with their diet for a longer period to see any progress. And even if you see quick results, they will probably be short lived unless you stick with the plan. It's the same with marketing. It's best to pick from a menu of possible methods. I recommend creating what I call a mixed plan. Having a combination of print and online methods has worked well for me and others I know. I consider Networking as the staple for a Real Estate business and then from there I recommend you layer on additional methods. Six months enabled me to develop my networking skills and begin to see a return on the investment of my time and energy. But when I say six months, I mean six months of two to three networking events a day, five to six days a week! From 7am breakfast events, lunch meetings and after hours mix and mingles. If you want to really maximize your opportunities, then going to a lunch once or twice a week will not suffice. The chances are that your efforts will pay you back many times over but you need the patience to stay in the game.

Money is gobbled up quickly by paid advertising so it's critical to track campaigns from the start. A small tweak in a headline can be the difference between an advertisement converting to leads or not. Consistency is key, but it would be madness to leave an advert running for six months without tracking and modifying. With online campaigns, you can see almost immediately whether an advert converts to leads. What takes longer is gauging whether a lead converts to a sale. You need to create a system to follow up with your prospects so that they don't go cold. Think of marketing like a funnel. You have all these different ways to attract people into your platforms, in order to qualify them. In simple terms, it's attracting as many of the right people to talk to about what you have to offer.

Now you've got the big picture I'll get into more detail so you can begin to create your own mixed marketing plan. It's impossible to market effectively if you don't know who your ideal client is. For this reason, it makes sense to begin by getting clear on the parameters of your target market. In the Real Estate business, we usually want to focus on regions because we work locally with clients. This is another reason why networking is a great method for meeting the right people. If business people attend local meetings, there's a high probability they have local business and live in the area. If business people who live in your region are the people you want to do business with, then this would be an example of your target market. You could further define your market by getting specific about what type of businesses or professionals you want to work with. For example, if you specialize in commercial real estate and want to attract investor types, it might make sense to target company owners with an aggressive plan of expansion in your area. If you specialize in investment or vacation homes, it would make sense to focus on people with a disposable income who are looking to buy a second home, or achieve a rental return on their investment.

How you choose to use social media will depend on your preferences and personality. I don't like to post personal updates because I'm a private person. That doesn't make it right or wrong. The main thing is finding the way of updating your chosen social media channels so that you can be consistent. Posting sporadically won't give you momentum so experiment to find what you're comfortable with and that way you're more likely to maintain your social media presence. It's similar with the social media platforms. Individual platform popularity will fluctuate as will your level of interest, so be flexible. Test out the different platforms and see where your ideal prospects are online. At the time of writing, LinkedIn is good for region specific marketing, so it could be a good option for you if you come to grips with how it works. It is very business specific, so is generally a good platform for all business people and doesn't lend itself to the personal as much as other platforms such as Facebook. I do not post anything that's unrelated to business. Period. I give very little insight into my personal life. I don't like to do it because it seems egotistical, but as I said, that's just my personal preference. Some people are talented at blending the personal with business to give their audience a taste of their personality. Modern marketing does benefit from portraying a personal brand, but whether you choose to create one around your personal identity, or prefer to stick to your company identity is up to you. Invest some time in looking at what other successful people are doing and get the flavor of the platform to see if it appeals to you.

It's essential to first define your ideal client. Once you know who they are, you'll be able to market much more effectively because every word of your marketing will be crafted with your model client in mind.

This is how you create a relevant marketing message. How you market will depend on where you can connect with these clients. Which platforms do they use? Which publications do they read? Which networking events do they attend? These are the basic questions you must answer in order to create an effective, mixed marketing plan.

My intention is also to help you to develop the mindset that will support you in your promoting. I'm not saying you must do this method or that method. It's entirely up to you what you choose because, there's no one right way to do it. What will work for you, may not work for me and vice versa. What is universal, is that you need several methods which work for you, because otherwise when one stops working, your lead sources will tend to dry up. It's never a good idea to focus only on one thing, because in this day and age, marketing changes fast. What works one year might not work the next. But the fundamentals remain the same. Marketing is just a way of getting what you have to offer, in front of the people who want it. It's a way of talking to people, and social media has amplified our potential reach. For this reason, it's more useful to point you to how marketing works, rather than what particular method works today. Once you know how modern marketing works, you can adapt to the latest platforms, publications and events. We're at a time in history where most businesses need to create their own marketing content. People want to be educated and helped to buy what they want.

66

Invest some time in looking at what other successful people are doing and get the flavor of the platform to see if it appeals to you.

99

I make videos. I write blog posts. I create my own content, which is shared on my social media channels. I have a virtual assistant who writes some of my content. This is something you can do too, but first get clear on your message and target market because otherwise you won't know what to say or write. You may decide to focus on only a couple of platforms, or you may want to go wide and post on multiple channels. There are tools to make it quick and easy to post and you can do it yourself or have an assistant schedule your posts for you. Again, it really depends on your preferences and financial situation. How much time do you want to devote to marketing each day? Do you have the budget to pay an assistant to take it off your hands? It's a good investment because you can focus on income generating activities instead, such as networking and following up with the leads that have already been generated through your marketing channels. But if you're just starting out and don't have the means to pay a virtual assistant, you'll need to wear all of the hats in your business until you get into profit and/or have a marketing budget. Scheduling posts in advance is a great method and helps you stay consistent when you are starting to build your brand.

Now let's give you an overview of marketing methods so you can create your own plan.

Mixed Marketing Plan Methods

Sphere of Influence

This is a good place to start for any enterprise. Your mother will say, "My kid's is a realtor." She'll tell her friends. We all know lots of people. Some of them will be well connected so it's not necessarily about who you know, but who they know. Many people in various industries get started in business, simply by telling people in their sphere of influence about what they're up to. Make it simple to refer people to you by keeping your message clear. Don't be tempted to pressure people into doing what they're not comfortable with, but instead ask them to spread the word in case they know anyone who may be looking for your kind of service.

This complements social media activities because you more easily stay top of mind when people see your updates. People do need to hear your message more than once for it to sink in. In many marketing sources it's typical that a minimum of six to eight "touches" need to occur before any potential prospect will convert.

By connecting on social media with people you know "in real

life," you will gently remind them of what you do and keep those touches consistent. Your closest contacts probably won't want to be on your newsletter list unless they are likely to also be clients, so social media is a middle ground to keep them in the loop, without having to constantly talk about your activities. Endless business talk can be a repellant, so keep your conversation normal and don't fall into the trap of only talking about your new enterprise, no matter how excited you are. Otherwise, you may find your sphere of influence begin to avoid you instead of support you. Ask what you can do for them first.

Networking

Building your connections will provide you with an invaluable opportunity to establish a strong foundation for your Real Estate business. Networking has the potential to have a bigger impact than education, marketing or anything else you do. Not only is networking a key component to success, but it also builds long term relationships when done well. This is key in any business, but especially in Real Estate, where we often benefit from referrals.

It is important to remember that networking is a mutually beneficial process. You never know when your skills and resources can prove to be beneficial to others in your network. Commit to be a great networker. The simplest way is to always be thinking about how you can assist someone else first. Ask yourself who you know that you could connect up with a contact you've met at a networking event. The law of reciprocity is a wonderful thing. By being of service to others, they are naturally moved to return the favor.

Social Media Marketing

The biggest reason Real Estate Agents need to be using social media to promote their business is to build their reputation. When you are able to position yourself as an industry expert, it will be a lot easier to attract new clients. Social Media is similar to networking in that the best way to do it is to think about what would be helpful to your followers. Don't try and sell directly on your own social media profiles, instead give useful tips and show that you know what you're talking about. The goal is to become the trusted professional. Ask yourself what would be of use to your ideal clients, and focus on sharing information which will encourage them to reach out to you to act as their agent. I recommend that you choose a couple of platforms and see which ones make the most sense for reaching your ideal clients. Get into the habit of updating your channels every day so that you develop a strong social media presence and people begin to notice and remember you. Again, it's all about consistency.

Unfortunately, the days of high visibility with free social media are over. Nowadays, you need to pay to play. There are big conglomerates such as Zillow and Trulia which are currently popular. I know brokers who invest $30,000 a month to generate leads. This type of advertising is considered social media because if someone looks at a house on Zillow and you're paying for an advert, your face will pop up as the agent to contact. This is an example of how you generate hot, paid-for leads.

I think it's a good idea to get used to running paid advertising early on in the business. At first you can't fathom paying thousands of dollars for marketing and advertising. But if you start with $500, once that starts to blossom, then in six months when you're doubling your business, $500 isn't going to shock you. And then in a year when you're seeing a greater return, a $1,000 won't be a big deal. It's something you have to buy into, both mentally and financially.

Print and Postcard Marketing

The most successful real estate agents in the country use a combined multi-channel approach that includes print marketing. The reality is that not everyone is tech savvy and many people still want to hold something tangible in their hands before they believe it's the real deal. A constant debate in marketing is whether print has become even more vital today because there is so much noise online. The point is to cover all of your bases and do whatever makes sense to reach your ideal clients, both online and in person.

I recommend you also incorporate marketing books into your reading schedule. One of my favorite books in this genre is *Words That Work: It's Not What You Say, It's What People Hear* by Frank Luntz.

This book offers helpful insights into how your choice of words and phrases has a significant impact in getting your message across. This is a critical skill for all types of marketing.

The Importance of Tracking

Once you've created your Mixed Marketing Plan, it's crucial that you put systems in place to track your results. Real Estate Agents often wonder which lead source is most effective at increasing their bottom line. Many find themselves chasing every new opportunity on the promise that it will attract new clients. The problem is they never get a concrete idea of what's actually working. Tracking is the solution. It's essential to track your marketing so you know what works. This sounds obvious but most people don't do it. With paid advertising, it's even more critical because you are throwing money away if it doesn't ultimately convert to leads and clients. Stop wondering and start tracking!

My Personal Psychology of Marketing

It's difficult to do anything 50% or 100% better. I'm just not that creative in marketing, and I don't want to reinvent the wheel. But if I can be 3% better in ten categories, then that gets me to 30% better performance across the board. This is the exact model I used when

Berkshire Hathaway acquired my company. My pens were just a little bit better than at other agencies. I didn't buy $1,000 pens, but I also didn't buy $1 pens. I bought $5 pens. I didn't order the cheapest business cards, but I didn't invest in $10 cards either. I chose $3 cards. I invested enough to stand out. I did enough to show better quality. But I did it everywhere.

As a chef, I know, if you hit the smell and the look but the taste and texture is off, you're screwed. But if you do everything well, you're golden. Visually it's beautiful. It smells good. The plate's hot. Then you cut into the food and the texture is perfect. The tastes all blend together like a culinary symphony. Knowing how to hit all of those components is the skill I carried from the culinary world, into Real Estate. When people see my marketing materials, I want them to think, "Wow, that is sexy." Being memorable matters in a sea of brokers in the Real Estate world. I employ all of these elements in my marketing to stand out and, historically, it has paid off.

When I made everything better, people couldn't resist. There's no point having a really strong marketing campaign but then you go to my office, and I'm in a hole in the wall. You come to my office, it's beautiful. It's modern. The décor transitions seamlessly from what caught their eye in the first place. I changed every door knob. I make everything a little better so when people visit, it's a wonderful atmosphere.

I'm selling a lifestyle. I'm selling an experience. When someone does business with my company, I want them to feel proud to be a client. I want to make my clients feel better simply by association with my brand. It's the whole package. I don't want there to be any type of confusion when a client is letting me represent them in a million-dollar transaction. I aim to be an accompaniment to what they already want to do. And not only are they going to pay me, they're going to enjoy paying me and doing business with me. This is how I market and how I operate.

Putting it Together with Heart Light

On a deeper level, everything I do with the marketing has to come from spirit and service. When you're of service, this is the law of reciprocity in action. When you channel service as your intention, versus, "I'm just going to do this to be the best or to make money," results are much better and everyone is happy.

You've got to love what you're doing. I didn't do it all only for my clients. I did it because I enjoyed it. I liked it. When I was putting marketing together in the early days, I relished in it, I would think, "Man, that came together well." Obviously, when you're spending money, you have to make sure that the people that you're creating the marketing for, feel that way too. But I really immersed myself in the process, and I looked at how people were going to receive it and whether they would appreciate the message. I asked myself, would they feel that what I'm trying to give them is of true value and service? This is how it ties into the spiritual part of how I do business. And people feel it. They don't know what it is, but something resonates with them.

A lot of work has gone into creating this experience for people, but it's genuine because I've developed these skills. I can truly serve as a mirror for someone, instead of judging or manipulating them for my own ends. I don't want to do that. At first when you're selling, you don't know completely what you're doing. If your intention is loving, you're less likely to be misunderstood, but you still need to develop your communication skills for business.

When you are confident in yourself, and what you offer, you don't need to hide things and people sense you are genuine. I want to give people what they deserve. Because I have no attachment to a certain outcome, I can walk away from a deal. That gives me so much leverage in any negotiation because people feel it. Knowing you're okay whatever the outcome, gives you true freedom and conversely makes the deal more likely to happen. I'm here to give value. I'm here to provide the best. But if someone doesn't like me or it doesn't work for them, I don't chase them. We can part ways amicably and move on. Now that's liberation.

In summary, I urge you to create or adjust your unique Mixed Marketing Plan. The Real Estate business requires a lot of action and there's never a better time than right now to start. If you're already established, what will you improve to create a better experience for your clients? Most importantly, whatever you do, do it with a sense of service and value. When you have no expectations, the universe tends to provide you exactly what you need.

Begin there.

[CHAPTER EIGHT]
FEAR–CONTROL–MASKS

> *The only thing we have to fear is fear itself.*
> **—Franklin D. Roosevelt**

ear is a lie. Fear is a chameleon. Fear is not real. Fear can be your best friend to help justify your shortcomings, such as why you didn't follow up on your Real Estate leads today, or it can serve as your worst enemy and pummel you further into despair when times are tough. Fear will always be a part of the human condition. Unless you're aware of how fear works, you don't realize when it's running the show. Fear has no fixed agenda, no bias, and no prejudices. Fear just is. It's an emotion like any other, but because our experience of it is typically negative, we tend to take it more seriously than when we feel happy or excited. We treat fear as a real problem, which is misleading because as we explored earlier, fear is an illusion. This means fear can enter our mind at any opportunity. Why? Because that is its nature. Fear feeds on itself, so if you are frequently anxious, you'll get more of the same, which then becomes a cycle of living in fear. The real question is how to develop a better relationship with fear, so it doesn't prevent you from reaching your goals.

The topics covered in this book are intentionally related to one another. The purpose of this chapter is to assist you in understanding how fear works, so that fear loses its hold on you, and therefore your encounters with fear naturally become more palatable.

John Lennon said "Life is what happens when you are busy making other plans". No successful business person I know has gone from point A to point B without some kind of disruption. The key to beating fear is to accept it. The trick is to train with it. The secret is to understand how it works. Treating fear as "a matter of fact" allows less opportunity for it to catch us off guard and call the shots. Although we never know how it will present itself, we know for certain that it will visit regularly. This understanding gives us something to rely on.

"Sweat more in practice, so you bleed less in war" is the mantra I embrace when facing my fears. When you look at how little we control in life, the weight of "what should be" can be replaced by the reality of "what is", which, when you accept the truth of it, is a weight off your shoulders.

Within the context of this book, here are some of the things we can control:

- What you say and how you say it
- What you eat and drink
- How much you sleep
- How you exercise
- How or if you act on your thoughts

These core activities in life are all, to some degree, within our control. We are able to make an effort to improve how we handle all of these things. Imagine mastering each of these and the impact it would have, not only on your Real Estate career, but on your entire life. The majority of people are pre-occupied trying to master things which are outside of their control, the "uncontrollable" factors. Investing our time trying to control these things, instead of the fundamentals, is why so many people fall short of what they desire to achieve. Becoming more balanced in the things you have control over, won't prevent fear, pain or tragedy. Nothing in life can do that. However, mastering what is within your control, does give you the best chance of being more resilient in mind and body, in order to recover faster. The simplicity of this, makes it frequently under-appreciated and overlooked.

Think of it like this. Who, when faced with a tragedy is likely to cope better? Will it be the person with a calm, healthy mind who eats a balanced diet, gets sufficient sleep each day, and exercises regularly, or will it be the person who neglects their health, feels high levels of stress and is always one thought away from a meltdown?

Thoughts pop in and out of our minds continuously. They're only thoughts; they're not real so we don't have to take them seriously. This awareness helps us to manage the ups and downs of life and business in a smoother way.

Hopefully, you now have a clearer idea of how fear works. But, more importantly it's what you do when fear shows up, especially in your Real Estate business. "Burning the clean fuel" I've referred to throughout this book, and embracing the elements of life which you have some degree of control over, is a major advantage that will assist you to rise above your fears and travel more smoothly on the road to success.

The following are common fears which I have encountered both in myself and others, when building a Real Estate business. This way you will be better equipped to deal with them.

Fear of commission-based income

For many people who have a traditional job background, the fear of only getting paid when you close a deal can be terrifying. This is why I recommend that if you're just getting started in Real Estate, you have at least one year's worth of income saved to cover your expenses, or have a part time job which covers your basic expenses whilst you launch your business.

If you are continually worried about closing a deal because it's the only way to pay your mortgage, your potential clients will pick up on your fear. It translates as neediness and isn't a smart way to start out. It's easier to operate when you are calm and composed, and know your bases are covered, whatever the outcome of a deal. The energy you bring into your transactions is key to making sales.

Fear of networking

Most people aren't comfortable networking and meeting new people outside of their existing circles. In order to grow your business and tap into new opportunities, you must engage with others, so the sooner you get comfortable reaching out to new people, the better. This is by far the most important aspect when growing your real estate business.

Once your network is established, you may be relieved to hear that the quantity of new people tends to reduce and the focus is then turned to nurturing and growing your most precious relationships. I have found that focusing on one dynamic person who consistently adds value and opportunities, can be ten times more impactful then constantly trying to meet more people. Quality over quantity is the key to developing a valuable network once you've connected with a substantial number of new people.

Fear of being criticized

The path of least resistance is to stand still and not "rock the boat", rather than to stand for something you believe in and risk criticism or disapproval. For this reason, it's common for people to swallow their dissatisfaction and sacrifice their own desires. People would rather be liked than rejected, but resentment frequently overtakes the ability to maintain the status quo. When resentment overflows, it contaminates relationships. I've found it's better to be yourself and walk away from others who won't accept you as you are, than to try and live your life to please them. In the end, all parties suffer because it's not sustainable to suppress your true self.

Fear of competition

In sales, competition is fierce. If you're not trying to get better each day and provide more value in your field, you will struggle to survive. Talent only gets you so far. It's those who push themselves further who have more chance of achieving their goals. When you train your mind, body, and spirit, in the way I'm covering in this book, competition dissolves because you are ready for anything. When you are ready, you become fearless.

Fear of working hard

If you take weekends off in the Real Estate business, you are either in a position where you can afford to, or you're naïve enough to believe you've chosen a job. If it's the second option, you will quickly learn that if you don't out-work the competition, you may be better off going back to a more traditional career. For many aspiring Real Estate professionals, much of the allure of the business revolves around the idea of a flexible schedule, and the opportunity to earn above-average income. Making a lot of money, consistently, can be difficult. This is just as true in Real Estate as in any other profession. The bottom line is, if you are fearful of throwing yourself into working long hours as you develop your skills, it will be a tough journey, unless you get lucky. However, accepting that hard work is a necessary part of the journey, significantly increases your chances of attaining each new level of success.

Fear of success

Many people fear success because they fear the price they think they'll have to pay. Achieving success takes everything you have, and usually more than you think you can give. This can feel scary. Going outside your comfort zone is the necessary ingredient to great achievement. The fear of change may also cause people to become complacent. Making up excuses and waiting for the "right time" can hold people back from taking the action they need to take to grow their business. That is why it is crucial to burn "clean fuel" and trust in your heart light. You'll begin to gain an awareness of when to take action and when to do nothing, as opposed to having your actions dictated by fear. When you feel secure in yourself, fear has less of a hold on you and you are free to take the action you're inspired to take. It doesn't mean you'll always win, however, the more chances you take, the better odds of success.

Risk versus reward

Years ago, I was on a flight to Miami to meet one of my NBA clients and I started chatting with a nice elderly lady who told me her grandson was also in the sports business. She said he was studying to be a sports agent for the NFL and she thought it would be great for us to connect. This type of exchange is a long shot, and could just as easily be a waste of time, but I always make a point to follow up on every lead and so I called her grandson shortly after I landed. And it so happened that he worked with one of the biggest independent sports agencies in the States. He was an intern, but he was only about six months away from taking his test to become a full-fledged sports agent. I mentioned what I was doing with some of my NBA guys and he told me about a networking retreat called Life Beyond Football, their company was going to host in Cancun. He thought I would be a good fit for the players and he put me forward. I had an interview and the organizers liked me.

Back then, I was a bit naïve because I didn't know how this type of event worked. I thought I would buy a plane ticket, pay for accommodation, and that would be it. Well as it turned out it doesn't work that way. They sent me an offer memorandum, with details of what sponsorship entailed. Suddenly I had a shot at the big leagues. But the required investment at that point in my career was just too high. I couldn't justify the figure, but I also couldn't justify missing out on the potential of the opportunity. I knew in my gut it was the right thing to do, even though the risk scared me. I decided to figure out a way to do it. At that time, I had barely begun to feel stable in Real Estate. I was doing okay, but was definitely not in a place where investing tens of thousands of dollars made sense to me.

And so, I negotiated and kept talking to them until I got it down to half of the amount, which was still a great deal of money.

I took the risk even though I was terrified and the reward was that the opportunity yielded many long-term profitable collaborations. I'm still in contact with the majority of the players. I've managed Real Estate investments for them and I've helped to counsel them on numerous other businesses.

The point I want to make in sharing this story is not that I advocate to blindly push through your fears; sometimes the thing that scares you isn't the right thing for you. Investing a boatload of money in anything doesn't guarantee a return on investment. Consider the individual opportunity carefully, and whether it's aligned with what you have to offer so that you have the best chance to maximize your efforts. If taking a risk feels right, then don't let fear get in the way of you doing your best to move forward.

Masks People Wear to Hide Their Fears

You'll encounter many different types of fears when working on your Real Estate business. Relationships are one of the Real Estate professional's most valuable commodities so it's a good idea to identify the masks people wear when networking. That way you'll be less likely to take things personally and be able to respond more effectively. I have also come to realize that when any of the personality traits in these examples bother us, ironically, it's because usually it's a trait we don't like in ourselves.

The shy, quiet, or reserved masks

Recognizing the difference between shy, quiet, and reserved is crucial. Some of the most powerful people are the ones who say little. Do not take their decision to listen more and talk less, as a negative sign. It may be strategic, in which case it's more useful to appreciate their style. Some individuals come across as shy and so it's useful to be kind and understanding. The best way to discern the difference, is by paying attention to their response. The quiet or reserved person's contribution to the conversation will typically be relevant to the topic. Whereas the genuinely shy person's response may be unclear because they're nervous. Focus your energy on each exchange and adopt a gentle non-judgmental attitude. Even shy individuals open up when they feel at ease. It is simply a mask some people wear to protect themselves.

The pompous, egotistical, or entitled mask

These masks can be difficult to deal with. However, when you understand that people adopt masks because they feel insecure and/ or are self-conscious, it makes it easier to have compassion. Remove the focus from yourself, and think instead about the person you're trying to engage with. It's never about you, so don't let your own insecurities get in the way. Egotistical people can be hit or miss in terms of the value of the business connection. Some people fall into the trap of thinking that the success they have achieved, warrants a superior attitude. You must be the judge of the level of their success, and whether dealing with this type of person is worth your time and energy. Some of these individuals may be valuable connections once you've got past the mask. However, some may not be accomplished, and only present themselves in this manner in order to throw others off the scent of their lack of achievements.

I have found that with kindness and patience, most people respond well because beneath the masks we wear, we are all just people who want to be appreciated. With each person, be mindful of how much time and energy you need to invest to develop a productive conversation, because you don't want to waste time networking with people who aren't a good fit for your business. A good way to smoke out the egotistical personality, is to listen to what others who you admire have to say about them. Legitimate networkers who offer value will consistently stand out. We are all legends in our own minds, so if you're unsure, just keep moving and put your energy where there's a good connection.

The know-it-all, can-do-no-wrong, not-my-fault mask

Anyone who thinks they are a master, doesn't need to announce it. True masters understand that learning is a life-long journey and only when you die will you stop learning. Again, hiding behind this identity is rooted in lack of self-confidence. The know it all, may offer snippets of insight from time to time, but make your exchanges quick and don't dabble in small talk. It can lead to wasted hours you can never get back.

The negative, judgmental, critical mask

This is another challenging personality. Individuals with this attitude to life may have been hurt by family or friends and thus see the human race as tarnished. They think that no one can be trusted and everyone is out for themselves. These negative type personalities can be useful in a business dominated by an overly optimistic demographic. Giving them your ear when all you see is good in any situation, will give you a different perspective that is worth evaluating. Other than that, spending time with negative people can be very draining and counter-productive to success. Always cultivate compassion and understanding, but it's usually a waste of time to try and convince them to be positive. I recommend you respectfully acknowledge their viewpoint and move on. Life's too short to surround yourself with negativity.

The comedian, trickster, funny mask

These masks are complex. Having the ability to make light of things does have its advantages. Helping people to feel comfortable often encourages them to disclose their innermost secrets. The comedian may use humor to divert their audience away from the facts. Regardless of their intentions, when you burn clean fuel, no trick will fool you for long. Standing firm with this personality type, tends to burn them out and either brings them up to your level of energy or they fade away of their own accord. If you don't give their performance much attention, it's unappealing for them to keep up the show. Of course, it's ok to have fun, but do know your limits and be aware that most of these personalities are not influential business leaders.

The aggressive, assertive, Type A mask

These types are difficult to ignore. It's best to show respect for their dominant approach or you will need to be prepared to be challenged. They are equipped to endure long, hard battles, so unless you have the stamina and the knowledge to back up your opinion, it may be best to avoid clashing with them. From the get go, assess whether your personality can mesh with theirs and if you can see yourself doing business with them. If the answer is a no, then I recommend that you quickly move on. There is no reason to waste your business building time with anyone if there's no valuable connection. Don't be surprised if they have similar thoughts and share them with you.

Quit now, suffer later

If you don't work on the holes in your game, your business and ultimately, you, will suffer. Get clear on what your weaknesses are and instead of avoiding them, embrace them and make a plan to improve. For example, if you're a great salesman but don't implement follow up systems, you could put your focus in creating the systems to maximize your sales skills. This will result in a huge pay off for you because you'll plug the holes of your leaky sales bucket. Or you might be great at attending networking events, but you have a poor diet which makes it difficult for you to reap the rewards of your networking because you're low on energy. It's challenging to sustain high performance when you don't feel at your best. Perhaps you work eighty hours each week, but don't make time to work-out. At some point, your body will get your attention and then you'll risk being out of the game for an extended period of time, due to ill health. This will cost you more in the long run, than taking time out to rest and reenergize your mind, body and spirit.

Putting it Together with Heart Light

You have probably noticed how fear always hovers behind the scenes no matter how much faith you may have. Navigating fear is an integral part of the human experience. The quicker you embrace this truth, the smoother the ride will be, on the rollercoaster we call life.

Balancing what you can control, whilst respecting what you can't, makes your heart light more potent. As a result of this deeper connection to something bigger than yourself, you'll be able to more easily identify and follow its guidance. Following your heart light will become second nature the more you practice and the more you realize fear is an illusion.

[CHAPTER NINE]
PRACTICE WHAT YOU PREACH–ACTION– MENTORS

here is an interlocking connection between practicing what you preach, taking action, and working with your mentor. I soon understood that for me to succeed in Real Estate I would have to embrace these three areas. Finding the right pathway often involves taking the wrong pathway first. This is not new, and yet, so many people in Real Estate get tripped up because, while they understand it, they don't live it. If you make "practice what you preach" your mantra, and you push yourself into "action", and follow my points on working with your "mentor", then I can assure you, your standing in your business community will grow exponentially.

My aim in this chapter is to ignite something in you, so that you take the required action to transform your Real Estate business into something substantial.

Working with a mentor takes time to develop. However, practicing what you preach and taking action, are instant changes you can employ. There is no substitute, you either practice what you preach or you don't, you can't hold back. It's all, or nothing at all. The same goes for your actions over thoughts, you do or you don't. So, let's climb into it.

Life is all about perception. What you process in your mind has the tendency to reflect in your life. In other words: what you think about is what you become.

I think that's why people are so shocked when their favorite athlete or celebrity, who "appears" to have it all, gets involved in a big scandal which goes against everything they publicly stood for. Or at least that's what they built their image and persona around. That is why doing what you say and maintaining that course throughout, is the key to sustainability.

Because (and this is the take away), in the end, your thoughts create your path. If you talk about how much you want to become the next biggest million-dollar Real Estate producer, yet in your mind you don't truly believe it's possible, your chances of goal fulfilment will be drastically reduced. Here's why; your thoughts wield more internal and external power than your spoken words. Self-sabotage is one of the biggest preventatives in human make up, it can quite literally stop you in your tracks. Making sure your inner mantra reflects your outer message, must become a defining principle in your life.

Congruency is a major factor in practicing what you preach. In simple terms, it means: what you say and what you do are the same, they are one. Naturally, our sixth sense, or our gut feel, is finely tuned and it can spot people who are not consistent. When we can't quite put our finger on why we don't trust somebody it's usually down to the fact that they are not harmonizing their actions and internal beliefs. All too often I hear people talking about things, in reality they can't possibly execute. So, remember, don't talk about something if you can't fulfill it day in and day out. You'll rapidly lose respect, and credibility, if you continue to default on how you're perceived.

We all possess the inner superpower (aka your Heart Light) to instantaneously detect somebody who has waded out of their depth on a subject they know little or nothing about. For me, it's a golden rule to only speak on topics where I have a wealth of knowledge because people can spot a fake very quickly and you won't be taken seriously again.

Passion and intent are a secret sauce that makes a fundamental difference in our level of success. However, your message and your action, if delivered without direction, make less of an impact. I'm certain you've seen emotional and passionate people in Real Estate who have fantastic intentions, but they are directionless. All their pent-up energy goes to waste.

When I hear somebody in Real Estate telling people how they are going to do this, and do that, my gut instinct is to say, "Show me, don't tell me." Words in the form of a public or personal declaration are valuable and important, but in time, the only factor that matters is your actions. Have you noticed how we are drawn to those people who get things done: the "doers". We tend to listen to people in our circle who just get on with "doing". Enthusiasm is good, but without the doing part, it's just noise. In Real Estate, getting a reputation as a "doer" is a powerful position to hold in your community, and business will follow. And the best part is that being action-oriented is directly within your control.

I've understood for a long time that you should work hard, communicate clearly, and always go the extra mile even when no one is watching. Anyone can turn it on for the audience, or in front of your office colleagues, but doing it when you are alone is one of the keys to success in Real Estate.

Always honor your word, even if it means taking a loss. Your integrity is what will impact people and they will never forget those instances for future business. It is said that "Your word is your bond", and in the Real Estate business nothing could be truer.

ACTION

People are creatures of habit. And the reason for that is because we all like comfort. It doesn't matter who you are or what you have accomplished, because the challenge in life, in order to grow and evolve, is to take action. In life, there will always be smarter people than you. Much smarter. Having brains helps significantly, however, your intelligence is wasted if you don't put action behind it. We are taught from an early age that knowledge is power; I've come to realize that action is power.

Real Estate demonstrates how action can be just as potent as knowledge. I am constantly encouraged by how many people who just work hard, day in and day out, constantly outperform the "smart" ones. They put the hammer down and get the work done, it's the shortcut to success, it's called "work". Having a plan is only as good as the action. Without action, even the perfect plan will flounder.

I've learned that action is the most important tool in your Real Estate business box, since moving forward (and making mistakes along the way) is far more proactive than standing still. You can't learn from being stagnant and you can only plan ahead so much. You can't grow more from what you already know. In life, as in Real Estate, it's rare that any plan goes according to design. Plans are fluid, and they need to be adapted to the changes they encounter. If you blindly forge ahead on your original plan, without being prepared to make mid-course corrections, you'll be off track and out of the game very quickly. Adapt or die. The time you spend overthinking something upfront is time wasted, rather than taking action. Action is the key. Remember, I'm not saying you should go into a situation unprepared. On the contrary, this can be just as damaging. We know the age-old saying, "fail to plan, plan to fail", and there is a reason we still hear that line, even though we've heard it countless times.

Like everything in life, finding a balance and learning to trust your instincts on when to take action, is the direct route to success. I've witnessed countless experiences in Real Estate and I can tell you why most people don't take action. It's not that they are unprepared, it's because they are scared of the unknown. I know that sounds simple, but it's true. Human's love certainty, we crave to know the outcome before we set sail. However, to succeed, we must embrace variety and accept uncertainty as a fact of life. In my experience, the reason we work hard, plan, study, and practice, is that when we do take action, we believe we have set ourselves up for success. Don't let your moment of action pass you by. In life, you must allow yourself to be prepared to take on the opportunity when it's placed in front of you.

The best methods I have found to propel myself into action are as follows:

1) Prepare tirelessly and become as skillful and informed as possible in your intentions. If your niche is single family properties, learn your market and all the details that encompass that sector. If you're a farm and ranch broker, then know your water and agricultural rights. If you are a commercial retail broker, then know what new developments are being built and why a new business should sign a lease there. When you are prepared, action is second nature.

2) Have a back-up plan, and a back-up plan for your back up plan. This is what preparation is all about. This is what makes successful people look accomplished. It's not that they are smarter than everyone else, or luckier, or more talented, it's because they have become masters of their craft. They are able to predict multiple outcomes (and prepare for multiple outcomes), and are able to adjust their approach, if and when it's necessary. The expression "business should be treated like chess, not checkers" fits perfectly.

3) Replay your actions in your mind as much as possible. The more you visualize, from start to finish, the more prepared you will be when it's time for action. Running the tapes of your day over and over, or replaying the meeting, or a recent transaction, or a positive prospect interaction, will form strong positive grooves in your mind. You'll create pathways of belief in your own actions.

4) Change your mindset to one of taking consistent action, and then jump into each challenge, fully present in the moment. If you know you're prepared and the only thing that is holding you back is fear of the unknown, then just go for it. As we covered previously, fear is just an illusion, albeit a powerful one. When you start embracing fear, you'll be surprised how quickly it dissipates, and before you know it, you've forgotten how fearful you were.

5) Be obsessed. If you don't live, breath and sleep what you do, then I urge you, do not question why you are not at the top of your game. To be obsessed means exactly that: full on, flat out. Remember, balance is subjective, however, proper eating, sleeping, and exercising should be incorporated as part of the definition of being obsessed. That being said, little else matters. Not because you don't care about anything else, but because you love what you do. Only the obsessed can understand another obsessive person. It's a unique club, but since I've joined it, I have never been more satisfied.

6) Be urgent. Although I assume "urgent" would imply taking immediate action, it's often not the case. In a world where speed matters and becoming obsolete happens in the blink of an eye, make sure that you are always pushing forward with a high degree of urgency. Time wasted on a great game plan can come back to haunt

you. For me, when I take action, I take huge, high-speed action, there's nothing like it.

7) It's better to ask for forgiveness than for permission. If taking action involves breaking the law, cheating, stealing, or anything else I missed, then of course I don't recommend this path of action. In history, great breakthroughs have come when action was taken, even when the plan, or the players, or the community, "were not ready". Waiting around for the planets to align, or the ducks to be in a row, or the pencils to be sharpened, generates more delay and more frustration, and results in deflated energy levels.

8) Ignore the haters. There will always be people who don't understand you, don't agree with you, and plain just don't like you. In my mind that's a good thing. You've heard the line, "if you don't stand for something, you'll fall for anything." I'm a walking billboard for that quote, it's so true. People step up to express their hate and displeasure only to those people who have taken action. If you don't take action, then the only person who will dislike you is you. Haters are also a great resource to help you see any holes in your game. Instead of defending yourself or bickering, take notes. I have probably learned as much from my critics as I have from those who applauded me. So, don't let what others think about you stop you from taking action. Let them hate, soon enough they'll ask you if you are hiring.

MENTORS

I thought a good way to tie this chapter together would be to talk about mentors and how important they are in your journey. Mentors, if respected and utilized properly, can help and prevent you from making mistakes that they have encountered along their own path. Having a proven mentor can pay you back in ways that money can't buy. In several instances, the advice my mentor has given me has proved to be priceless. The clarity it provided helped me take action and get out of my head, out of my fear, and out of the unknown. My mentor had been in that situation before and only his experience in that precise moment helped give me what I needed.

66

Mentors, if respected and utilized properly, can help and prevent you from making mistakes that they have encountered along their own path.

99

I was in the middle of an ugly business divorce. My partner at the time, had decided to turn an inability to compromise, into a justification to serve me papers to break up the company. During the ordeal, it felt like a very weak and destructive action. I was in a situation where my employees' jobs were in jeopardy and the past several years of gruelling work, and time, was being threatened. Not to mention the fact that my career and company were in danger. Needless to say, it was not a good situation. My first thought was to sell, regroup, and build again. However the reality was that my partner was not in the financial situation to pay what the business was worth. However, I was. What to do?

This is where my Mentor came into play. As a seasoned Real Estate mogul (for over 40 years), developer, and owner of dozens of ranches, hundreds of commercial properties, and with a net worth in the hundreds of millions, he has seen quite a bit. I explained to him my situation and expected to have to wait at least a few days, or at least a week, in what, in my mind I thought was a huge dilemma. As quickly as I stated my case, my mentor had an answer. He told me, I should buy out my partner. He gave me the why, the financial perimeters, and his opinion on how to best negotiate during mediation. At first I was in shock on how fluid, rapid, and clear his response was. It was hard not to doubt him, but, based on his stellar track record I gave my reluctance little thought.

During negotiations through mediation, everything my mentor had told me to expect, came to fruition; from my ex partner trying to inflate the price (knowing I had more financial leverage), to how my counter proposals slowly put me in the driver's seat. In the end the negotiations concluded and I had prevailed as the sole owner. Within two years I had completely recouped what I paid, and I had tripled the company's growth. We became the number one rated firm in the city and I have already had several offers to acquire my company for over ten times what I paid. In the end, the advice from my mentor saved me hundreds of thousands of dollars and will ultimately make me several millions of dollars. Pretty good for a ten minute phone call.

The moral of this story is that an experienced mentor in your field is priceless and if the relationship is respected and cultivated, your potential opportunities are increased exponentially.

Mentors should be respected and cherished. While speaking with your mentor, talk little and only ask questions when appropriate. As I mentioned in my story, my mentor is one of the biggest developers in the state and his net worth is well into the nine-figure range. When he makes time to advise and educate me, I always make myself available (no exceptions). If you want to grow faster than your competition, then having a mentor is an essential part of your development. Having a proven mentor to advise you, typically opens up opportunities for more deals. It's not a lie when people say that the people you surround yourself with, form a big part of your growth. So, knowing this, you would be foolish not to want to bring a highly successful mentor into your world. There is no cap on the number of mentors you can have. Although, if you are lucky enough to find one who is dynamic, one tends to be enough.

My rules for working with a mentor are as follows:

1) Choose a mentor who is in your industry and who has a proven track record. You need someone who knows what you are going through and someone who knows what you are going to face.

2) Always make your mentor your number one priority. If this means cancelling a meeting, or several meetings, then do it. Your mentor provides more value to you than a meeting which can be rescheduled.

3) Don't ask your mentor to call you. This is a big pet peeve and shows a lack of respect for their time. Remember, your mentor doesn't need you! It is not a two-way street.

4) Don't disagree with your mentor. They are not giving of their time for you to brainstorm. Only if they ask you for your opinion should you voice it.

5) Listen to every detail. Record everything, take notes and learn from listening. A mentor's advice and their opinions are nuggets of pure gold.

6) Go above and beyond when your mentor asks you for anything. In the Real Estate world when my mentor asked me to deliver on any given task, I always went over the top: always. From providing the best comparables, to gathering more information about a deal. I didn't do this to impress my mentor, but to show how serious I was. When it was my time to be given an opportunity, it was clear I could be trusted.

7) Stay in touch with your mentor. Good mentors are typically extremely busy. It should not be their job to keep up communication, that's your job. A text message or email is encouraged and a way to show your mentor respect. Continuous contact is simple and it keeps you in your mentor's thoughts which is priceless.

8) Accept the challenges (all of them) your mentor sets you as an opportunity to grow. Whatever the situation, it's always in your best interest, especially when your mentor is pushing you. Embrace the challenge and know it's for your betterment.

9) Be grateful and give thoughtful gifts as a sign of appreciation. To some of you this may sound like brown nosing, but in my experience, it's almost impossible to buy something for someone who is worth several hundred million dollars. Think about that for a minute! Therefore, the point is in the thought behind the gift and not the value of the gift. That is why listening to details is crucial and confirms to your mentor that they correctly chose you to mold and teach.

10) Don't ask your mentor for anything that you are not willing to stand by, or which may be a risk. Your word is your bond, your word is everything, and it's well worth noting that it can be destroyed in an instant. Before you bring any kind of business dealing to your mentor, make sure it's well vetted. Even after that, make sure everything is fully transparent and they have the opportunity to see the whole picture. If you wouldn't do the deal yourself then never take the deal to your mentor.

11) Have skin in the game. A mentor respects your ability to get involved. It shows you are truly in and ready to go down with the ship! You gain much more respect once you enter this realm.

The old adage, "Money talks and BS walks" really sums up the real players from the big talkers. When other people's money is on the line, the money can be an afterthought. Things start to get a bit more serious when it's your hard earned cash in jeopardy. A great experience where I learned this to be true was again with my mentor. I had told him how gung-ho I was about getting into developing apartments and that if he knew of any deals worth pursuing that I should be one of the first calls he made. Well, the power of intention was in full effect and within a week I got the call. My mentor had found a deal, so good, that if cash was not brought to the table within twenty-four hours, it would be gone! I ran the comps, surveyed the area and indeed, at the cost the sellers were asking, I could easily double my money - just on the land alone.

However, the catch was that he asked if I wanted to finance the land and he would then help fund the rest of the build. These are the moments where character and opportunity are built. From the outside looking in, it appeared to be a no brainer. Right? Double your profit instantly, based on equity, real estate, and with a mogul backing you. What is there to lose? But until you are in those shoes, bring a substantial amount of cash to the deal, it's never that easy, or at least it wasn't for me. But that's the point. The difference between success and mediocrity is having skin in the game. No risk, no reward. Pull the trigger and be a hero, or pass up on opportunities and stay where you are.

So, I went for it. Twenty-four hours later the cash was in escrow and we closed a few days later. That was the first of many such experiences and I'm happy to report, I have done well on the vast majority of deals I went for. I don't think these transactions are ever easy, but the thrill of the deal is what keeps me coming back. It also proved I was all in, and had hefty skin in the game. At that point there is no turning back and it insures you work as hard as necessary to make sure you make your money. Respect is earned, not given.

Putting it Together with Heart Light

When you have faith that everything happens for a reason, it's easier to take action and to practice what you preach—confident, that what you are doing is bigger than yourself. Having faith, helps to push you beyond your fears, gets you out of your head, and into action. I also think it helps you to attract the right mentor into your life, at the right time; one who can help guide you on your journey. For me personally, knowing that my purpose is deeper than making money, enables my heart light to direct me down the right path. I hope you can see how your own unique spiritual connection can be the foundation of every aspect of your career and life.

[CHAPTER TEN]
EMOTIONAL INTELLIGENCE–SACRIFICE– FINAL THOUGHTS

66

Educating the mind, without educating
the heart, is no education at all.
—Aristotle

99

n today's Real Estate world, it's not advisable to ignore others and
think you can accomplish great things alone. As technology becomes
an integral part of everyday life, it's easy to neglect the human
touch. From automated social media posts to autonomous cars, there
is very little we will have to do manually, as we race into the future.
The human trait that will remain crucial to success is our level of
Emotional Intelligence. This is widely considered one of the most
essential commodities and valuable skills for the new age of business
generation.

People with a high emotional intelligence quotient typically have
increased self-awareness. When you understand that your feelings are
neither right nor wrong, but are simply an unavoidable and intrinsic
part of being human, it becomes easier to see a situation from another

person's perspective. In times of crisis, having a clear grasp on why and how people react when they feel insecure, gives you a major advantage. Instead of reacting emotionally to their reaction, you have the awareness to take the time to process developments and decide what to do, if anything. Instead of defending your position, you can reason and compromise. So much time and energy is wasted when there is a lack of emotional intelligence on either or both sides. This is why it's crucial to develop your EI.

Another key attribute of those with a high EI or emotional intelligence quotient, is their sense of timing. When you're tuned into the people around you, you intuitively know how and when to respond. There have been so many situations where I have been in meetings or social exchanges and I have engaged with individuals who have no clue when the appropriate moment is to get their point across. When ill-timed, the situation can be awkward or inappropriate and both or all parties become confused. Even worse, the individual who doesn't have a high sense of EI may become angry or frustrated and blame others for the poor timing. This is a common trap many get caught in. Less is more. There have been numerous instances when, holding my tongue, no matter how badly I had the urge to speak, was a better choice than getting my point across. Words can always wait to come out of your mouth, however, you can't retrieve them once they have been dispatched. Consider your response before speaking or you may regret it.

Having a high sense of EI also enables you to behave with integrity. Instead of being a "yes person" and going along with the crowd, you have clear boundaries and preferences. Your values dictate your decisions and when you operate in accordance with them, it naturally creates a sorting system which turns off the people you don't mesh with and attracts the ones with whom you are a good fit. Your heightened EI has a direct correlation with your Heart Light, which, as we've covered throughout the book, has the ability to guide you on your path. I don't think it's a coincidence that the doors of life open more frequently when your EI is heightened. It's like having superpowers at your disposal, so please use them wisely.

> **Words can always wait to come out of your mouth, however, you can't retrieve them once they have been dispatched.**

A great way to develop your EI is to watch and listen to people. Pay attention to how they move. Are they fast and always in a rush, or are they slow and ponderous, maybe they have an injury which slows them down? How do they talk? Are they clear and concise, or scattered and talk over you? What is their appearance? Are they neat with tidy nails and pressed clothes or are they unkempt with wrinkled clothes? When you put yourself in others' shoes, in an effort to understand them, versus interpreting and drawing conclusions solely from your biased point of view, patterns emerge. You begin to understand why people act as they do. When you have a greater understanding of what makes people tick, it's easier to respond with compassion even when you don't agree with their viewpoint. People will want to be around you more, and will volunteer more information when you listen to them and they don't feel judged. In life and business, a high quotient of emotional intelligence, gives you a major advantage because good relationships are at the heart of every endeavor. When you display empathy, and learn to speak other people's language, difficult relationships and situations often transform, as if by magic. "Problems" vanish and "impossible" people disappear, to be replaced by a better version of themselves. How you interact with people, determines how they show up. You can only ever see someone from your perspective, so by expanding your EI, your ability to see what's going on behind the various masks people wear, deepens. As a result, you are better equipped to allow people to express who they are, and they begin to trust you and open up more freely.

Being aware of your body also helps to sharpen your connection to your innate EI. When you feel good, you naturally perform better. At the other end of the spectrum, when you neglect your health, the opposite may be true. Looking through this lens helps you to quickly adapt to the shifting terrain. For example, if someone is sick or upset, you would have more patience, and would adjust how you engage accordingly, without the need for drama.

EI is a fundamental part of creating productive relationships which are the key to a successful Real Estate business, so it's worth every moment you invest in developing yours.

SACRIFICE

"If you don't sacrifice for what you want, what you want becomes the sacrifice."—Unknown

Nothing great comes easily, or if it does, it typically needs effort to maintain. Anything worth achieving requires dedication. This is why there are so few "masters" and why most people end up floating about aimlessly. One of the biggest lies is thinking that the road to mastery will be easy or it will ever come to an end. The day you stop growing, is the day you start to die. Each day you wake up, you can say yes or no to something new and in saying yes, you give it attention, which encourages it to grow. What that something is, each time you make a decision, will be the key factor to achieving your goals. The first significant step for the rest of your life starts when you define your purpose, then the real work can begin and sacrifice is required.

As you work towards your goals there will always be some type of sacrifice. The question will be, is what you are sacrificing, worth what you want to achieve? If the answer is not an instant yes, then you may want to reconsider your purpose. If you fixate on the destination and final outcome, and have a difficult time enjoying the journey, you may want to reconsider your current path, especially in Real Estate.

Creating jobs and financial freedom for my family was, and still is, my purpose. My book's purpose is to help you, the reader, to evolve into a more fulfilled person and Real Estate professional. The driving force for writing this book wasn't for it to be a bestseller. Writing a book takes huge sacrifice. It took a significant amount of time, energy and money. The hours, days and years it has taken for me to turn my idea of becoming a published author into reality, came with a price. Longer work days ensued. Instead of writing, the additional time could have been allocated to building my Real Estate company. On many occasions I sacrificed family time, to be locked in my office, as I attempted to finish another chapter. But my why remained clear and my heart light was strong and constant throughout. Moving forward, through each sacrifice, is easier when you're guided by your heart light.

I don't believe there is any "final level" of sacrifice. With each new achievement, there will always be another sacrifice. Just because you get over a major hurdle doesn't mean there isn't another one to cross. I recommend you look at your achievement as a gift which prepares you for the next kick in the ass! All jokes aside, the faster you change your mindset regarding how you perceive sacrifice, the more elegantly you will be able to handle it. When you are aligned with your purpose, take heart in knowing that your sacrifice confirms you are on your true course. Each time I'm faced with the next step, I instantly choose to keep moving. Having that mindset helps to dissolve the emotional resistance you may feel about giving things up, and it becomes just a normal part of the process to achieve what you want.

To me, sacrificing has become a game. The more I give up now, the more I tilt the odds to achieve my long-term goals. This mindset has helped me to become very disciplined, not only in my Real Estate career, but in all areas of my life. When you perceive your life as a whole, you start to make each decision with the intent to align with your bigger purpose. It's not enough to sacrifice your weekends and to work long hours. As we've already covered in detail, working on the quality of your diet, sleep, and relationships, will make you a force to be reckoned with. This message is what I have done my best to impart throughout this book. Being willing to make sacrifices in service of your bigger purpose, allows your heart light to shine and your clean fuel to burn at its brightest. As you sacrifice, you eliminate the distractions which previously held you back. When you accept sacrifice as an integral part of the climb, the weight you must carry is significantly lightened. My advice is for you to enjoy your journey, your purpose, and your why, whilst doing your best to be fully present in each moment. The life you have been given is in the present, even though your long-terms goals are, by their very nature, in the future.

Putting it Together with Heart Light

The fact that you were drawn to this book, tells me that you desire to activate your most prized possession: your heart light. I've been aware of my heart light since I was a child. It has guided me through the highs and lows of life and has always been the driving force in my decisions. As the world gets smaller and moves faster, embrace your own heart light, and realize that it is always present within you, to show you the way, both in how you practice Real Estate and how you live your life. In so doing, your interior world slows down, no matter the circumstances around you. You become calmer, the sacrifices make sense, and your clean fuel burns with a steady flame.

Final Thoughts

To conclude, I want to thank you for deciding to sacrifice your time by reading these pages. My desire is that the time and attention you have dedicated to this book, provides you more insight and clarity on time tested principles and how they can easily be applied to your daily Real Estate career. I hope you take some nuggets from my hard-won experience of life and in the Real Estate world. Whether your goal is to close hundreds of millions of dollars in Real Estate, or you are just starting out in business, follow your heart light.

In the end, when your purpose is clear, life tends to give you more than you could ever ask for. This is my dearest wish for you.

www.ingramcontent.com/pod-product-compliance
Lightning Source LLC
Chambersburg PA
CBHW071859090426
42811CB00004B/670